Superhighway to Wealth

Kristy S. Phillips, J.D.
&
Kathleen B. Wilde

Superhighway to Wealth
by Kristy S. Phillips, JD & Kathleen B. Wilde

Printed in the United States of America

Information Directions, Ltd.
470 North University Ave. #203
Provo, UT 84601

e-mail: arss@InfoDirect.com

68Q25432 WW

Contents

Introduction 7

Section I - Internet Background 13
Chapter 1 - History 15
Chapter 2 - Demographics 17
Chapter 3 - Size and Growth 21
Chapter 4 - Disappearing Domain Names 25

Section II - Why the Internet? 29
Chapter 5 - Company Image — Prestige 31
Chapter 6 - Way of the Future 33
Chapter 7 - Globalization — The Great Equalizer 37
Chapter 8 - Faster and More Accurate 39
Chapter 9 - Cost Savings 43
Chapter 10 - Low Overhead 47
Chapter 11 - Increasingly Accessible 51

Section III - The Internet Marketplace 53
Chapter 12 - Online Business 55
Chapter 13 - Communications 57
Chapter 14 - Telecommuting and
        Audio/Video Conferencing 63
Chapter 15 - Research, Collaboration
        and Development 65
Chapter 16 - Marketing, Pricing, Ordering, and Sales 69
Chapter 17 - Customer Support 75
Chapter 18 - Processing an Internet Sale 81

Section IV - Tools 87
Chapter 19 - World Wide Web 91
      Home Pages 93
      HyperText Markup Language (HTML) 94
Chapter 20 - E-mail 99
      E-mail Addresses 100
      Mail Lists 100
      Mailbots 101
      Listservs 102
Chapter 21 - Gopher 107
Chapter 22 - FTP 113
Chapter 23 - Usenet 121
Chapter 24 - BBSs and Online
      Commercial Services 127

Section V - Business Ideas for the Internet
      Spark Your Imagination 133
Chapter 25 - Business 137
Chapter 26 - Education 143
Chapter 27 - Management 147
Chapter 28 - Marketing.. 151
Chapter 29 - Needs-Resource Matching 155
Chapter 30 - Service 159
Chapter 31 - Computer and Technical Services 165
Chapter 32 - Keys for Success................................ 169
Conclusion 173

Glossary 177

Appendices 185
Appendix 1: Demographics and Statistics 186

Appendix 2: Places to Advertise on the Internet 187
Appendix 3: Business and Business
     Related Listservs 190
Appendix 4: FTP Sites 192
Appendix 5: Bulletin Board Systems
     that Allow Advertising 193
Appendix 6: Sites Related to Tax Issues 194
Appendix 7: Subject Related Internet Addresses ... 195

Index 203

Superhighway to Wealth

Introduction

The business and financial worlds are in the midst of a revolution that will change the world. This is not a revolution that topples governments, but it is bound to break down the barriers of time and distance, barriers that have cost businesses millions. This revolution is being led by the great advances in computer technology and the explosive growth of the Information Superhighway, the global network called the Internet. This network of networks links millions of people throughout the world. It is the most powerful communication resource known to man. It acts as the confluence for the knowledge and technology for our time. Colonizing the new world, the land rush, the gold rush, and the space race were all significant opportunities, and many people became very rich, but nothing in history even compares to the wealth, opportunities, and freedom available to you on the Internet. It is simply the single most powerful marketing tool in the world.

The age of electronic commerce is waiting to be

exploited. Although computer technology has been around for years, we are at a crucial point in our development as a society. Futurists have predicted that the Information Superhighway will have an enormous impact on the way we live and work. It's happening now. Currently there are over 30 million people around the world using the Internet. Internet growth over the past three years has averaged an increase of more than 200,000 percent each year. State and national governments, schools and libraries, businesses and individuals are discovering that they can access all types of information from all over the world. That information can be in the form of text, pictures, even video clips - anything that can be digitized. And it can be brought to our homes or offices in minutes.

We are truly on the brink of an electronic era that will change the world. Think back at how new technologies have affected lives. When the printing press was invented, the elite, the rich, passed laws that prevented the public from accessing this new technology called books. The rich kept the books for themselves to assure their elite position in society. They knew that if they could keep the knowledge to themselves, they would control the wealth and maintain the power. As a result, it took hundreds of years before everyone could read, and when they could read, the wealth of society became more evenly distributed. Similarly, for forty years, only the rich and powerful had automobiles. For thirty years, the telephone was a tool of the elite. The television was held by the elite for maybe only twenty years. The computer was held by the elite, the rich, the powerful for one precious decade - ten years. In fact, many

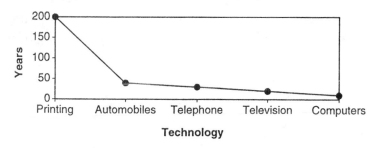

How Fast Technology is Accessed by the General Public

people were duped by the argument that they didn't need to learn how to use a computer. The majority bought the argument that only smart, special people could use or could even learn how to use the computer. Many became afraid of the computer. Today, the fact is, you have to know how to use the computer to work in a store, use the library, get money from your bank account, or do countless other things. The rapidity with which the invention and implementation of new technology is increasing means that if you wait to embrace a technology, you will quickly be left behind.

The computer has changed our lives for the better and made more people millionaires than any prior technology. In the days before everyone started to use the computer, some ordinary people, people just like you and me, saw its potential. In just a few years, Bill Gates, an obscure college kid, became the richest man in America and built the same type of fortune it took the Fords, Rockefellers and Kennedys generations to build. Today physical, economic and financial survival are increasingly dependent on cutting edge technology. Gates says that the fortunes made on the Internet may

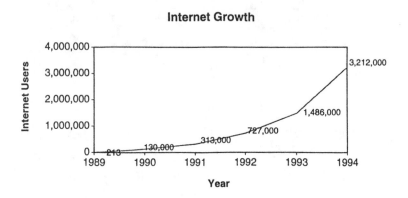

Internet Growth

surpass his, and that they will be made even faster by people that have never been heard of today. Why shouldn't that be you? All you have to do is learn the Internet and have a good idea. You cannot afford to delay. The powerful only held the computer for one decade. Currently only 45% of homes in the U.S. have computers, but it is predicted that the Internet will be in nearly every home by the year 2003. The time to move is now. Technology development is moving faster and faster, and you have to be quick to take advantage of the Internet. He who hesitates really will be lost.

Section I

Internet Background

Chapter 1

History

The Internet has been around for more than twenty-five years, but the general population is just now becoming aware of it. At first it was the domain of the researchers and academics, and access required knowledge of complex computer language, but this is no longer true. Everyone can now access the Net. No one "owns" the Internet, and no one "regulates" it. There are a certain number of "conventions," but even these are being tested and changed. Though the academicians would like to continue to dominate the Internet and control its information and power, it isn't going to happen. Too many people are becoming familiar with the Internet and its applications.

		KEY WORD SEARCH	
Year	Internet	Information Superhighway	Internet & Information Superhighway
1990	1,540	16	4
1991	2,994	87	16
1992	4,671	98	13
1993	9,085	2,970	356
1994	32,295	18,198	4,125

The Net is being publicized in a growing number of talk shows, newspapers, and magazines. Look at the Key Word Search table. This table shows the number of articles in which the word "Internet" was used during the last five years. The public is fast becoming aware of the Internet, and whether we like it or not, it will soon be an integral part of our lives.

Chapter 2

Demographics

There have been few comprehensive demographic surveys taken about Internet users. This is because the Internet is rapidly growing and evolving. Dynamic growth makes it difficult to describe exactly what the Internet is and who is on it, but we do know a few things. From the few voluntary surveys that have been conducted, we know that the majority of Internet users have been male, under thirty, have a high degree of literacy and a reasonable amount of disposable income. The profile of the "average" user describes the academic environment of the Internet that until now has been primarily colleges and research universities. Students, faculty members, and scientists were the ones who had access to the Internet. During the early 1990's, the National Science Foundation, the government organization trying to develop and maintain order on the Internet, relinquished their stranglehold on the system and began to allow commercial use. Since then, the growth of the commercial population of the Net has been nothing short of astounding.

As more and more people connect online, the

picture of the "average" Internet user is changing. By mid-1994, the percentage of professionals on the Net had risen to 45% of the total number of users, and for the first time, students and faculty became a minority of users with only 43% of the total. The group that responds to these surveys continues to be those who are well-educated and progressive. They are the kind of people who are willing to invest in their future by getting connected to the Internet. They are the kind of people who have a vision of what the Internet can do for them both personally and professionally. What will the average Internet travelers of the future be like?

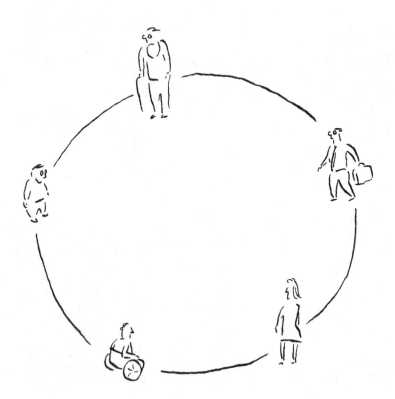

They will be male and female, children, teens, and adults. They will be Fortune 500 companies (there are almost 300 of them on the Net now), small entrepreneurs, students, senior citizens, doctors and librarians. The Internet will still be an invaluable tool for research and communication, but it will be available to everyone. The small businessman will be able to compete with the large corporation.

It should not be surprising that the business segments of the Internet are the fastest growing, and that literally thousands of new-to-the-net businesses go online each month. Smart businesses are working now to reach those who access the Internet. Internet users represent a whole new market, and these businesses realize that now is the time to take advantage of that market. The fact is that the Internet has the capability of reaching more people than any other technology and at a significant cost reduction. Sales letters, order forms, brochures, newsletters, sound bites, video clips, and product updates can be sent to hundreds of thousands of people — instantly— for pennies. It is easy, fast and convenient. Contrast Internet marketing to traditional mediums! Previously the number of people reached was proportional to the amount spent. With access to the Internet, this is no longer true. The fabric of the Internet is currently being tested and stretched. The Internet that takes shape will control the future. This means that now is the time to make your contribution to its development. Any business, no matter how large or small, stands to profit from the Internet. Where else can a global market be reached so inexpensively and efficiently? No matter what your product or service is, the time for doing business on the Internet has arrived, and the technology is here. To succeed, your business needs to be on the forefront of this new technology.

Chapter 3

Size and Growth

The population using the Internet is growing at an almost exponential rate. It consistently doubled in size every year between 1988 and 1992. Then in the spring of 1993, Mosaic, an Internet accessing program which made using the Internet easier, was introduced, and growth went crazy. Statistics indicate that in 1993, traffic on the World Wide Web, a specific realm of the Internet, was measured at 443,931% the amount of the previous year, and those who advertised over the Internet more than doubled in number from 19,664 to 42,883.

It is estimated that there are somewhere between 30 and 70 million users of the Internet worldwide. The growth of individual Internet users is amazing, but so is the growth of commercial users. As of November 1994, there were 25,000 commercial domains on the Internet, and there are 1500 to 2000 new companies connecting every month. Not everyone is traveling on the Information Superhighway yet, but these significant growth trends are hard to deny. More and more people are discovering the possibilities of electronic communication. It is estimated that if

current growth trends continue, by the year 2000 close
to a billion people will be on the Internet.

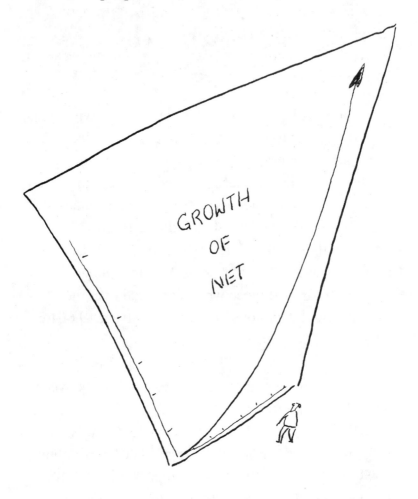

Electronic shopping for both products and services
is also going to expand exponentially as more and
more people discover the convenience and the value of
using the Internet. Even now you can order everything
from the groceries to legal advice, fancy chocolates or

complete electronic books on the Internet. You can find a translator for your overseas business without ever leaving home. If you have skills and expertise that can be valuable to others, with just a few key strokes on your computer, you can tell the whole world about them. In a few hours or a few days you can receive requests for your products or services from all over the globe. The Internet growth rate is so rapid that any information which is published about the Internet is outdated by the time it reaches the press. Don't be discouraged. With an Internet connection, current demographic figures will always be accessible. See Appendix 1: Demographics and Statistics.

Chapter 4

Disappearing Domain Names

Leaving the statistics behind, the Internet growth can be demonstrated under purely practical circumstances. Domain names and addresses are things that businesses on the Internet will need to obtain to identify themselves in cyberspace. Consider the following: if you applied for a domain name in 1994, it was issued in a few days. If you call to obtain a domain name in 1995, you will be told that there is at least a four-week wait. The wait is long because more than two thousand domain name applications are being filed every day. You can apply for domain names through your local provider or through an organization called InterNIC, which assigns and keeps track of all domain names in the United States.

The domain names consist of a series of letters and/or numbers. The actual address is the part that falls after the @ symbol. People can find you on the Net by typing in your domain "address." You choose the name that goes between the @ and the name. The code name (com, gov, edu, org, or net, for example), indicates whether you are a business, a government site, or a school, etc. Sometimes there will be numbers and letters combined with dots, slashes or underscores after the com, gov, edu, org, or net to indicate a pathway to information on the host computer. It is important to note that the address must be copied exactly, because Internet addresses are case and spelling sensitive. In the Internet address, ww@infodirect.com, the domain name is infodirect.com.

The final portion of the domain name which follows the last period is more specifically called a top-level domain (e.g., com). Breaking down the domain name, ww@infodirect.com, will give you an idea of how it works. The company name is Infodirect and the .com portion of the domain name is a that describes Infodirect as a commercial business. Other common top-level domains include the following:

	DESCRIPTION
edu	educational institutions
gov	government
mil	military
org	miscellaneous organizations
net	network organizations

Internet addresses that belong to foreign countries usually have a two-letter which follows the three-letter name. For example, 'ca' identifies Canada, and 'jp' identifies Japan. Currently the top-level domain found in every Internet address is not always a correct description or indication of the location or organization, etc. For instance, some commercial businesses have .org or .edu as part of their addresses. This is because domains are used by the computer to identify the chain of responsibility for that computer system's connection to the Internet.

Smart business owners are applying for a domain name now. Since there is only one name per user, once a domain name is claimed, it is gone, even if it happens to be a copyrighted name in the real world. When the name Wendy's is issued, it is gone. First come, first served, and we don't mean just hamburgers. If cousin Wendy applies and is issued the name first, it is hers. Some individuals are currently registering for prominent domain names in hopes of selling them in the future to the company that operates under that name.

Progressive companies have begun placing their domain addresses on all of their letterheads and advertising. Companies are including their Internet addresses on billboards. Savvy shoppers can purchase that company's products over the Net, and the business presents itself as up-to-date and dynamic. That's the kind of company that has a loyal customer base. Domain addresses provide another excellent way for an organization to build name recognition and a ready connection with the public. A name has a powerful influence when marketing a product. Like a clever or descriptive 800 number, an easy-to-remember domain name will plant itself in the minds of consumers and make that company or that product the most familiar, the easiest to contact, and thus the most likely product to be purchased. A domain name will be easier to remember if it is closely associated with the company's name or one of its well-known products. A recognizable domain name will enable your company to take advantage of the Internet market, present the appropriate professional image, and make money.

Section II

Why the Internet?

Chapter 5

Company Image—Prestige

Imagine what a presence on the Internet can do for a company's image! Companies on the Internet are perceived as dynamic, powerful, on the cutting edge. Customers view them as the leaders in their respective industries. Progressive businesses are the ones to be reckoned with. This image will command respect and attention from prospective customers and competitors and sales will increase.

The Internet provides immediate access to customers in ways that are fresh, new, and convenient. Your company will be perceived as one which cares about its customers and is willing to use the latest technology to best serve them.

We recently spoke with an associate who interviewed with a Japanese company that does a large amount of business in the United States. This company does not yet take advantage of the communication and information resources of the Internet. During the course of the interview, the company representative made a point that there would be many late days spent at the office because of the ongoing need to communicate with engineers and other people involved in the manufacture of the product. Ongoing communication is essential because the products are not standardized, but are specially made according to customer specifications. Imagine the time and money that could be saved if that company could communicate with its customers and designers over the Internet! No one would be left out of the information loop, because there is essentially no cost to sending messages or holding bulletin board or real-time conferences. The savings on telephone calls and faxes alone would be staggering. Design changes could be handled within minutes. Approval for projects could be given immediately.

Our associate was astounded that the company didn't have an Internet connection. It is hard to believe that an otherwise advanced company, so dependent on research and development and ongoing overseas communications, isn't connected. This point alone caused our colleague to perceive the company as behind the times and unprogressive. Once your business is on the Internet, take time to let others know you are there. Cultivate a dynamic image for your company; it will pay off.

Chapter 6

Way of the Future

The Internet is the best way for businesses to capitalize on the market of the future. Values are shifting and lifestyles are changing quickly. Almost every aspect of life is affected by the rapid technological changes occuring all around us. The Internet is the logical tool that businesses can use to adapt to consumers' changing wants and needs.

Consider the following. In the last few years, the number of women working outside the home has jumped from 42 to 58 percent. Seventy percent of women with children under the age of six hold jobs. Time is priceless for these women, and traditional store hours are inconvenient for them. They welcome alternate shopping sources that enable them to spend precious time with their families and shop on their own schedules. They appreciate the hundreds of databases, support systems, and forums that help them keep current in their fields. These resources are available to them at very little or no cost over the Internet .

The number of older people in America is growing. Seniors like to shop at home for many reasons that include not having to hassle with parking or traffic, or worry about slippery roads and sidewalks. With the Internet, seniors who do not or cannot drive, who fear bad weather, or who hate public transportation, won't be kept from doing their own shopping and interacting with others. They will enjoy the dignity and independence of being self-sufficient. With the Internet, declining health will not stop seniors from being able to take care of their own needs. There are so many products and services that would be of value to the senior market. Have you thought of maintaining a Bulletin Board System for seniors, making available electronic catalogs for online shopping, offering a wide selection of large-print books, providing tax and retirement tips in downloadable files, or planning travel arrangements and tours geared to this group?

Many consumers miss the personal touch selling that has all but been eliminated from traditional department stores. Today's retail marketing has moved to high-volume discount stores with little or no concern for customer relations. Lower prices have been achieved, but consumers are increasingly complaining about rude service and the lack of variety and quality products. These consumers enjoy shopping from the privacy and comfort of their own homes where they can "browse" at their leisure, yet be able to communicate quickly with a human if they want further details, a different size, or special handling. Merchants can provide the kind of support that customers yearn for and that will keep them coming back. The cost to the merchant is negligible.

In 1990, marketing statisticians found that 98.6 million Americans made shop-at-home purchases, and annual sales of goods and services through direct marketing topped $200 billion. Seventy percent of consumers have used an 800 number for home shopping in the past 12 months. We are talking about traditional direct marketing methods. Imagine what will happen as more and more people begin to use the "highways" of the Internet! A look at these facts makes it obvious that the time has come to alter marketing concepts to fit with America's altered lifestyle and enjoy the financial rewards that will be the by-product.

Chapter 7

Globalization — The Great Equalizer

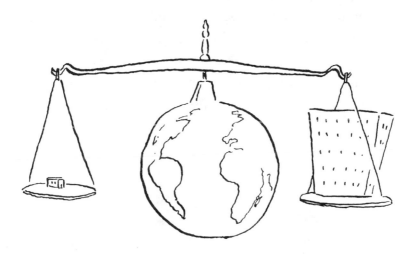

For the first time in history, any company with Internet access can participate in the global economy. The Internet has leveled the playing field between large and small businesses. In the past, only large companies were able to leverage their resources so that money could be invested in seeking after and opening markets worldwide. Internet access shortens distances and ignores national boundaries, allowing small companies to increase visibility from local to global instantly. Small and large companies alike share resources without regard to size or asset base.

Businesses located in any area, no matter how remote, can compete internationally and can access information, resources, and customers that only large companies could approach in the past.

The competitive advantage associated with being a large and diversified company is shrinking. However, the competitive advantage associated with the ability to cut costs and reach unexplored markets by using the tools of the Internet is there for all. The companies and businesses who connect to the Internet now will be the ones to attain this competitive advantage.

Chapter 8

Faster and More Accurate

The Internet offers an instantaneous market. Computers can help us work faster and more efficiently, and that is one of the beauties of the Internet. Consider for a moment the time it takes to run a traditional direct mail campaign. Once you have designed the original ad, you must take it to a printer to be typeset and printed. This process takes at least a week if you are lucky, usually longer. Next you take the pieces to a mail house to be stuffed and addressed. Again you must add another week. Once these pieces are put in the mail, you are at the mercy of the Post Office. It is realistic to find bulk mail pieces that arrive over a month after they were placed in the mail. The Post Office recently quit guaranteeing that priority mail will be delivered within two days. First class mail generally takes two to three days if it is in-state, longer if it is out-of-state. This means that traditional direct mail takes about a month to reach the consumer. Publication ad campaigns, such as magazine ads, are also time intensive. Once you have designed the original ad, you must take it to an artist to be converted into camera-ready art. Next you send it to be published. The deadlines for ads to be submitted are often two to three months prior to actual publication, so this process is generally more time consuming than a direct mail campaign.

Advertising over the net can take less than twenty-four hours if you choose to do the whole process by yourself. The nice thing is that it is not so technical that you can't accomplish the task on your own. Even if you choose to hire someone else, the whole process can be accomplished within a few days. Creating a home page for your business, composing well-written electronic brochures and sales letters that can be sent to hundreds of interested buyers within a matter of minutes, investigating appropriate newsgroups where you can tell others about your product and/or direct them to your home page on the World Wide Web, and preparing downloadable documents for those who wish to retrieve information are business tasks which you can do yourself or hire out.

One of the best things about the Internet is how simple it is to update information. You can quickly and easily add or delete an item in a catalog or change a price. It is just as easy to correct an inaccuracy or mistake. Why is it that no matter how many times a layout is proofed there always seems to be a mistake? On the Internet, you can quickly and easily make corrections or update your information without any additional cost or delay. The faster you can contact potential customers, the faster the money can start coming in.

Chapter 9

Cost Savings

The best part of doing business over the Internet is the savings. E-mailing your friend in London, or 30,000 business acquaintances in Japan is as cheap as calling your friend next door— it's free! Money that you spend on long distance charges, postage, and paper is saved. The fax will no longer be used to send documents because different Internet tools will allow you to send or make available any size of document to customers, colleagues and suppliers. Internet communications are efficient because they take place whenever or wherever people have the time or want to communicate. Busy signals and phone tag will be eliminated. There will be no need to worry about whether the fax you sent is readable, or if it was actually received on the other end. Time is money, and the more efficiently your time is spent, the more money you can make. Travel is one of the most obvious time and money wasters in today's global economy. With the Internet, online meetings will replace many out-of-town conferences and meetings. Also, as technology for audio and video conferencing becomes more developed, the need for out-of-town or international meetings will dramatically decline.

These same reasons make the need to commute to the office less necessary for many individuals. If their job descriptions do not require them to be at the office and they have the ability to communicate and download anything that can be put on a computer at their fingertips, why waste time traveling to and from work? This also allows companies to invest less money in large and expensive offices. Money previously spent on travel and office space will be seen in company profits.

Today's businesses invest a tremendous amount of time and money on research and development. The Internet is the most valuable resource of information this world has to offer, and what is more, you don't have to leave your home or office to tap it. Businesses can use the Internet's resources to quickly gather information from colleagues, experts, and large organizations such as government and universities located all over the world.

As customers become more demanding and markets are more defined, market research has become another necessary area in which businesses invest their money. Market research on the Internet can be very effective because people naturally separate into discussion groups and forums according to their interests. Market research can take weeks, months, or even years using conventional research methods, and it can be costly, depending on how the research is conducted. Traditionally, data has been gathered through mailed questionnaires, personal interviews, phone interviews, observation and other methods. Using the Internet, you can observe discussion groups and in the process analyze the interests of hundreds of people simultaneously. Relationships can be developed via the Internet, the most important being your customers. Interviews and discussions can be conducted with random potential or actual customers, no matter where they are located. These can be conducted one-on-one or in groups by using different Internet tools. Learning to use the Internet in these ways will undoubtedly save considerable money.

Businesses spend billions of dollars annually on TV, radio, magazine, and newspaper advertising to reach consumers. Although such advertising mediums vary greatly in terms of cost, they are all very expensive in relation to the Internet as an advertising medium. Advertising on the Internet can be done very effectively for a much smaller investment, primarily the cost of connection. If you are marketing products or services on the Internet, you will want to become familiar with the World Wide Web (WWW). The WWW features home pages which act as virtual stores or catalogs in cyberspace. To effectively market your product or service on the Internet, you will probably want to set up a home page.

Costs associated with creating and maintaining a home page through an access provider run between $200 and $300 a quarter. Amounts and time periods may vary. The true measure of cost, however, is in relation to the number of people reached by the advertisement. With a traditional direct mail piece, the postage alone costs more than $300 to reach just a thousand people one time. The same $300 investment in a home page, with the proper links, will allow you to reach literally hundreds of thousands, perhaps millions of people, on a daily basis for ninety days. Considering the numbers of people reached, there is no comparison between the cost of advertising over the Internet and that of traditional advertising.

Chapter 10

Low Overhead

The cost of running an Internet business is minimal. When thinking about getting online, there are several things related to cost that you will want to consider. First of all, you will want to get the connection that will give you all of the tools and access you need to improve your business and save you the most money. If all you want is limited Internet access and e-mailing capability, then you will no doubt choose a different access provider than the person who wants unlimited Internet access and the ability to use all of the tools of the Internet. Access providers are people who have spent money on hardware, software, and phone lines so that others can find their way onto the Internet without investing a fortune or becoming a computer genius. You might not be confident in your ability to setup and use the resources of the Internet unless you have a local provider who is close-at-hand to offer technical support.

One thing is certain, you will want an access provider that is only a local call away. If your provider is not local, then you pay long distance charges for all your communications including your Internet connection. For example, our company connection is with a local provider who is connected to a large server that is connected to the world. (Keep in mind that a national or online access provider can be a local call away, if they have a local or toll-free number for you to use). Whenever we send e-mail, we send it locally through our local provider who then takes responsibility for transferring our message to a large server which then relays it to the world. Thus, each time we e-mail somebody, no matter where that somebody is, it is only a local call. If you were paying long distance charges for all of your e-mail communications, the cost of using the Internet would rise sharply. As the infrastructure of the Information Superhighway grows, this may not be a problem in the future with more access providers moving into rural areas.

There are a variety of ways to obtain access to the Internet, but they are all different in regards to cost, services provided, and flexibility. There are generally four different ways to connect to the Internet. Three of these ways involve gaining entry onto the Internet through access providers. There are local, national, and online access providers, each of them charging slightly different fees and offering different services. The fourth is to become your own provider.

Each access provider will charge a monthly fee

along with a charge for hourly use over a specified limit. Local access providers are people in your own community who can connect you to the Internet for around $30 per month. They will allot you around 50 hours of free Internet usage before charging any hourly fees. The monthly fee of a national access provider will be about the same as a local provider, but they will only give you around 30-40 monthly online hours free. The charge per hour over time usually ranges between that charged by a large online service and a local provider. The monthly charge for using a commercial online service will only be around $20. However, they will only give you around five hours of free Internet access before they begin charging you $2.50 to $3.50 per hour over the connect fee.

When you talk to a provider, you may only want a single user's account that provides one e-mail address. A commercial account that provides additional e-mail addresses will require an additional investment. Such accounts allow you to send and receive all the e-mail you want as a non-commercial account. Depending on the provider and your computer, most accounts allow you to use FTP (file transfer protocol), gopher, telnet, chat, and other tools of the Internet and give you access to the World Wide Web. Obviously, the more user accounts you have, the more it is going to cost. If you don't mind all of the incoming e-mail going to one address, then a single user account will be sufficient.

If you are large enough, you may wish to consider becoming your own provider, but it does require a large investment in money, knowledge, and time. This method also requires a commitment to the continual maintenance of a computer system. Costs associated with setting up a system like this will vary somewhere between $35,000 and $250,000, depending on your hardware needs. Becoming a provider will also require that a T1 or a T3 telephone line be installed which will cost about $1,000 per month. No matter which way you choose to connect, remember that the Internet will make your work much more productive and efficient.

Chapter 11

Increasingly Accessible

Originally, to communicate on the Internet you had to use the computer language UNIX, but with the enormous growth in practical applications of the Internet, several easy-to-use interface software programs have been developed to enable communication in a point-and-click environment. Mosaic and Netscape are programs that allow a complete computer novice to cruise the Net with relative ease.

There are also text editors such as HyperText Markup Language editors (HTML) that help businesses establish electronic storefronts on the Net. These programs are easy to use in a Windows or a Mac environment, and a knowledge of a computer language such as UNIX is not needed. Using an HTML editor, you can place your company name, logo, and what services or products you have to offer in an easy point-and-click setting for millions of people to see. If they want to know more, they contact you electronically or by phone. Contact can be made with those truly interested in your products or services without the normal constraints of time or distance. You can service your customer in Australia as cheaply and easily as the customer across town. These new programs enable the smallest home-based businesses as well as the largest corporations to benefit from the Internet. Best of all, Mosaic, Netscape and innumerable other software programs are available on the Internet for free! More and more competition between businesses will be based on quality and service rather than on how much money is spent on advertising.

Section III

The Internet Marketplace

Chapter 12

Online Business

The business segment of the Internet is growing at a tremendous rate. Each month more companies realize that they must have a presence on the Internet to effectively compete. With the Internet more than doubling in size every six months, home pages, e-mail, and hypertext are becoming the buzz words of this decade. As a rule, it is the business which does everything faster and cheaper that finds the greatest success. Businesses large and small are going online to maximize their profit potential.

Utilizing the global resources of the Internet will be the key to the future success and longevity of a business. The Internet offers almost limitless reference sources for research on technical data, as well as market demographics, in a fraction of the time and cost of traditional methods. Market testing can be done with minimal expense. And if your idea is right, the financial rewards can be substantial.

Not only Fortune 500 companies, but also many home-based entrepreneurs are using the massive communication capabilities of the Internet to gather information about what the public really wants and to tell them how to get it. Newsgroup discussions give a feel for what sort of information, products, services or skills people need. Improvements in products and services can be made more quickly because customer feedback is *fast*. Advertising costs go down because you can get your message delivered to hundreds of thousands of potential customers with just a few keystrokes on your computer. Your expertise can be valuable to more people than you ever dreamed you could contact.

How the Internet is Utilized

Today many businesses are using the Internet in numerous ways. The Internet acts as a multifaceted resource with instant connectivity and global communication. With the speed and diversity of the Internet, every company should quickly be able to find several applications that will contribute to enhanced business success. Some companies discover value in an Internet connection from communication savings alone, but there is so much more than e-mail. The impact of the global communication on research and education has already been so profound, that the Internet has been dubbed by many as the second Gutenberg revolution.

Chapter 13

Communication

The Internet was originally developed to insure uninterrupted communication for the government. Today communication is still one of the core strengths of the system. Businesses use the Internet internally to keep departments, work groups and individuals in close contact, and externally to keep in touch with sales representatives, suppliers, information brokers, and customers both nationally and internationally. Communication with government agencies, the academic community, researchers, and the public can help any company enhance its business. What better way is there to keep current on the latest trends in marketing and science? Think of the time and costs savings! Mail and phone bills will be slashed, yet communication will be enhanced. Just imagine—no more busy signals or playing phone tag.

E-mail is the backbone of Internet communication. Using e-mail is a great way to exchange information with anyone at anytime. It is much quicker, cheaper and more efficient than postal mail, often referred to as snail mail. There are other methods of communicating over the Internet. IRC

(Internet Relay Chat) makes possible real time communication. It requires the appropriate software, but it allows individuals to type and receive messages to and from others instantly. At the present time, much of the "talking" on some IRC channels is meaningless,

e-mail   snail mail

but the possibility is there for unique business applications. Private conversations and conferences limited to invited guests are available. With IRC, company personnel in far flung places could conference together live. If your company requires video or audio conferencing, the capability exists, but is very expensive because of the equipment, software, and the amount of bandwidth required to send such messages. Improving technology and competition should force these prices down in the future. It should not be long before audio and video conferencing will become a popular alternative for out-of-state meetings with colleagues and customers. Individuals can work anywhere and still communicate. Imagine the travel expenses your company can save, how much more productive your personnel will be, and how the potential for reaching a larger market will encourage business growth. Schlumberger is a powerful example of a company that is successfully using Internet communication.

Schlumberger

Schlumberger is a multinational company operating from more than 2,000 offices, field sites, and research centers located in more than 100 countries. Schlumberger's focus is in the petroleum industry where it provides oil field services to various sites all over the world. The company also manufactures measurement systems used by gas, water, and electric utilities. Because of the high-tech nature of Schlumberger's products and services, and the distance that often separates them from their many work sites and customers, the implementation and application of communication technology have always been a priority at Schlumberger.

The Internet has been the critical tool for improving networked communications for over a decade at Schlumberger. Their commitment to the Internet is evidenced by the hiring of an internal

Internet expert whose job it is to initiate the education and training of Schlumberger's employees about the Net through the development of tutorials and workshops. Reasons emphasized in the workshops for using the Internet to improve work tasks include the following:

- communicate with customers and colleagues through e-mail

- transfer research and technology findings among colleagues

- download software

- conduct research

- buy software and order parts

In particular, Schlumberger has had success using public domain software that is available on the Internet to finish projects instead of creating their own software from scratch. The company has found that the developmental stage of projects is completed more quickly if public domain software is utilized, and there is no extra cost.

Schlumberger has experienced the power of having access to the Information Superhighway and is committed to maintaining its leadership role in today's globally competitive environment. They plan to stay abreast of new technologies such as video and audio capabilities that will allow them to integrate the Internet even further into their business.

Chapter 14

Telecommuting and Audio/Video Conferencing

In the last few years, the government has urged companies to use employees who telecommute from their home offices in an effort to save resources and control pollution levels. Vice-president Gore sets an example by holding press conferences over the Internet. The reporters and journalists type their questions on their computers, and Vice-president Gore types the answers on his. Both the questions and the answers appear on all of the participants' screens. It is a press conference in real time, but the location of the participants is irrelevant.

Businesses have found that employees enjoy working from their homes, and they also are more productive. Businesses also improve their bottom line by not investing capital in larger offices. This trend of telecommuting is bound to grow as companies realize the potential of the Internet. Employees can keep in contact with colleagues and clients and obtain company information, just as if they were at the office by using FTP and other Internet tools.

As the prices of bandwidth drop, audio and video conferencing will become a more viable and popular alternative for long distance meetings with colleagues and consumers. First-time customers are more comfortable working face-to-face with suppliers when putting together important deals; video conferencing can bring customers and companies together in a comfortable and convenient manner saving time and money. Multinational companies will benefit tremendously from the ability to audio and video conference with colleagues from different countries. Companies will find it easier to assimilate operating procedures as they make the way business is done worldwide more consistent.

Chapter 15

Research, Collaboration and Development

The foundation of the Internet is the staggering amount of information available for immediate access. Passage to databases, books, and manuals that contain things such as research results and training information is available at the touch of a button. What's more, the information is usually free. Besides electronic newsletters, databases and archives, experts in many fields congregate and discuss their specialties on the Internet. They question each other and share research results. What better way to gain new insights and responses to research questions and to track the competition? Science and research data are available to everyone in large quantities. The Internet provides businesses a functional way to become more competitive with a minimum investment. The increased access to state-of-the-art information on products, materials, and new ideas keeps personnel aware of emerging technologies and evolving markets. Many businesses use the Net as a problem solver. Instead of hiring an expensive in-house expert, employees can use the Internet to locate and speak with experts. Company research on every level will be enhanced with little or no additional expenditures.

Companies collaborate over the Internet in order to gather resources, information, and expertise not available in-house. As companies focus their resources toward technology specialization, the need to share and borrow in the creation of new product development becomes more and more apparent. Several companies have recognized the power of working with suppliers, colleagues, and business partners via the Internet to complete tasks. Software can be shared, downloaded, and tested over the Internet from any location worldwide, as long as there is an Internet connection. Greenville Tool and Die, a relatively small company in Michigan that manufactures automotive sheet metal stamping dies, has had success working with software suppliers via the Internet.

Greenville Tool and Die

Greenville CAD (Computer Aided Design) programmers have found that the Internet saves time during software design and implementation. Greenville obtains software from a variety of sources that are also connected to the Internet. When there is a problem with software, Greenville can work in conjunction with software suppliers via the Internet, saving enormous amounts of time as opposed to solving the problem using conventional communication methods. Greenville downloads the software from their supplier over the Internet, tests it, and then reports back any problems. And it's all done over the Internet. Greenville CAD programmers can then work online together with suppliers to correct the problem. In an industry with very short lead times, the Internet is a valuable tool in keeping Greenville ahead of the competition.

Greenville Tool and Die has also had success using the Internet to conduct technical support, download software patches, and locate high-tech information. Greenville has been particularly impressed with the global connectivity that the Internet provides. One example of this occurred when Greenville downloaded public domain software and had questions about how to incorporate the software for Greenville's purposes. Greenville e-mailed their questions to the provider in New Zealand and received a response to their questions the next day. Greenville was amazed at the global connectivity the Internet provided, and they were even more amazed to receive such a quick response from a provider of free software.

Chapter 16

Marketing, Pricing, Ordering, and Sales

Marketing over the Internet is conducted by thousands of companies from a variety of industries for three main reasons. First, there are millions of people who access the Internet every day. Second, the costs associated with reaching these millions are minuscule. Third, Internet marketing is an attractive marketing alternative because it is easy to identify and locate a target market interested in your product. The ease of finding groups of people with specific interests, beliefs, tastes, etc., is unique to the Internet. People on the Internet naturally separate into discussion groups and forums, called newsgroups, according to their particular interests. By studying the conversations of newsgroups and participating in mailing list discussions, you can find groups of people who will be interested in your product. In fact, by listening to them and addressing their concerns, you can probably come up with new products that they need and will be easily marketed to them. Take a look! The target market of your interest has probably already been identified and segmented for you.

Internet marketing is different, however, and does require a slightly different approach than conventional marketing. Keep in mind that there is no single approach to marketing a product over the Internet. The important thing to realize is that the environment and culture of the Internet are dynamic, always changing. Thousands of people are finding their way onto the Information Superhighway for the first time every day, and with this rapid growth comes change. Many Internet pioneers would have you subscribe to their definition of netiquette (how you should conduct yourself in 9), but limiting yourself to their protocol might leave you out-of-touch with the emerging Internet world and groveling in your competitors' cyberdust.

Not only is marketing much easier, but communicating with suppliers and vendors over the Net is also quicker. It increases the effectiveness of ordering, pricing, and stocking inventories. In addition, the Internet can also help a business convey important bids or cost estimates more effectively than traditional mediums such as the telephone, fax, or express mail. No more telephone tag or dealing with FAX machines that have problems transferring long documents, and which can be difficult to read. Communication is instant and accurate.

Express mail is great for delivering important

information, but when critical decisions are pending, a quicker, more reliable medium is necessary. E-mail is the perfect alternate method. Many suppliers and vendors offer customers direct electronic access to pricing and ordering information to facilitate the ordering process and to lessen the likelihood of customers seeking other suppliers. However, being connected to a single supplier can limit a company's flexibility to contract with other suppliers that offer better terms, prices, and delivery. This will no longer be a problem as more and more suppliers connect to the Internet and make prices and quantities of their goods available online. Businesses can shop around for the supplier that will offer the best prices and delivery terms. Inventory levels will not be a mystery, and ordering will become more efficient. The Internet allows global connections with numerous suppliers, thereby magnifying company flexibility. The availability of this kind of information can be crucial in helping a business stay competitive, reduce costs, and avoid stock outs.

The potential of reaching millions of people at a minimal cost is enough to convince even the most conservative marketers to gain access to the Internet. Soon, every business in the world will be utilizing the resources of the Internet. That's why it is imperative for businesses to connect now and learn the culture and tools of the Internet. Tools that an Internet marketer must learn to use include the following: newsgroups, bulletin boards, online providers (either the big ones like Prodigy and CompuServe or a local one that you can dial-up or telnet to), the World Wide Web with its home pages and hypertext links, gopher, FTP, and e-mail. These tools can be used individually, but if used in coordination with one another, a business can realize more fully the potential of Internet marketing. Learning how to effectively use each of these tools will help a company establish a recognizable presence on the Internet. The Country Fare's Internet presence has bolstered its customer base.

The Country Fare

The Country Fare (**http://country-fare.com/cf/ home.html**) is a small eatery grossing less than $500,000 per year, located in Palo Alto, California that has used the Internet to advertise. When the eatery analyzed the local market, they noticed that there were thousands of people who worked at computer companies who had Internet connections at work and at home. Realizing this, the restaurant decided to set up a World Wide Web site, complete with their menu, daily specials, and a map to guide customers to the establishment. Since creating their Web site, business has picked up considerably at the restaurant. Restaurant partner Bill Lynch believes the Internet is the most viable advertising channel around for promoting the restaurant.

You can see how Internet advertising can help establishments such as The Country Fare which relies on walk-in business at a particular site; imagine what Internet advertising can do for an organization which is not restricted to serving customers from a specific location, but that reaches out to a global market and serves its customers wherever they might be. Remember that your Internet advertisements, whether you intend them to or not, will reach people all over the world.

Chapter 17

Customer Support

The Internet is revolutionizing who does customer support and how it is conducted. Now companies can communicate with their customers in ways that they could only dream about in the recent past. Businesses do not have to invest large sums of money in stamps, envelopes, paper, or telephone lines. Instead they can contact their customers by electronic mail. Quality customer support will be a viable service which can be offered by all businesses. Companies can communicate directly with customers in fresh and innovative ways. Personalized marketing is the way of the future, and customers will demand a direct link with companies.

In today's market, governed by demanding customers, fierce competition, rapid product cycles, and increased segmentation, customer reactions and communication are essential in finding ways to attract and retain customers. Customers with access to the Internet will no longer have to wait on the phone because *all customer service agents are currently busy.* Instead, they can e-mail their questions and complaints and receive a quick response. Customers will then be able to read the response to their questions at their convenience. In addition, customer complaints will be addressed more efficiently with the right person answering the question the first time instead of being transferred again and again. Customers will not have to call back several times to get in touch with the right person; their e-mail will be directed to the person with the right answers. Good service is good business, and good business translates to profits.

Companies will also be able to conduct product research by monitoring the after-purchase attitudes and thoughts of their customers. Remember that every customer can be reached by e-mail with only a few keystrokes. Businesses will not have to invest in telephone or mail questionnaires in order to gather important information for product research and development. Effective research on customer satisfaction and use is the catalyst to discovering improvements for current products and the springboard for new product ideas that will be in demand. Recall that e-mail is electronic mail — stamps are not required, and response time is brought to a minimum. Needless to say, tremendous amounts of time and money will be saved.

Electronic brochures containing order forms can also be sent to customers to inform them of new additions or new products. Customers can fill out the order form and purchase the product using electronic cash. The ability to electronically transfer money online has been developed and companies such as DigiCash and CyberCash continue to improve the technology. This kind of direct marketing will soon be done by all companies, not just large direct marketing firms.

On the Internet there are also mailing lists or discussion groups where customers can voice their complaints, compliments, insights, desires, and ideas about products. This is an innovative and effective method of discovering customers' needs. Consumers can also be directed to the organization's home page where they can find general information about the company and any other information the company would like to convey. Businesses can use all these tools to form an alliance with their customers. Consumers with access to the Internet will appreciate how it keeps them in touch with what their favorite organizations are doing — in essence, customers and organizations will become partners in business, forming a lasting relationship that will ensure the organization's continued stability.

When it comes to closing the distance between themselves and their customers while improving customer service, Federal Express is setting the standard and is way ahead of its competition.

Federal Express

Federal Express is the world's largest express transportation company. They deliver 2.2 million items to 192 countries each working day. Not only is Federal Express the largest parcel delivery service in the world, they are the technology leaders in the express carrier industry. Federal Express was the first to install computers in vans, provide sophisticated automation in the mail room, and develop tracking software. Federal Express has always done its best to be in the forefront of the business world and apply the newest technology to their express delivery service. Because of this attitude, Federal Express is the premier express carrier in the world.

In January 1995, Dennis Jones, chief information officer at Federal Express, said, "We're leading the industry down the information superhighway . . . Last month almost 70% of our volume originated through automated technologies. With the general availability of FedEx Ship and our Internet presence, we're confident about reaching our goal of conducting nearly 100% of our business online."

In an effort to achieve this goal, Federal Express has set up a World Wide Web home page on the Internet (http://www.FedEx.com). This home page provides users with up-to-date news and information about Federal Express services and allows them to track the status of their shipments. January's home page gave information about FedEx Ship, which is new, free-of-charge desk-top shipping software. This software allows customers with personal computers, modems, and laser printers to complete and print their own air bills and call for courier pickup. Soon customers will be able to download FedEx Ship from the home page. Federal Express also plans to make individual or corporate services and billing information accessible via the Internet.

Chapter 18

Processing an Internet Sale

An essential ingredient of any marketing program is fulfillment. Fulfillment means "to promptly carry out, accomplish or satisfy promised conditions." From a marketing standpoint, fulfillment has a deeper meaning: "to strengthen a company's market." Good fulfillment means satisfied customers, enhanced business reputation, and increased profitability. The Internet truly improve company fulfillment by speeding delivery time and thereby increasing customer satisfaction. Customers can order products over the Net, and the orders will be fed directly into the company's computer database which allows instant processing.

Billing — It is important to decide how to handle billing over the Internet. First you must decide between prepayment and billing. Marketing experts have found that there is generally better response when a company fills the order and then bills. These experts admit that there is a sizable risk from customers who do not pay, but the sales benefits often outweigh the loss. If your company decides to take this billing risk, it should be well organized. It is important to send out invoices at the time of shipping. If the original order is not paid, follow-up invoicing should be quickly processed and sent.

Prepayment — If you decide to run on a prepayment basis, you need to know that payment over the Internet presents new challenges. Both consumers and merchants demand an automated system to take advantage of the speed of electronic commerce. Originally, payments made for products seen on the Internet were sent by mail. These early payments were slow in arriving, delaying processing time, and thereby holding up the transaction to the point that some Internet benefits were lost. Credit card payments, though quicker, originally presented security problems. When a credit card number is given over the Net, there is a security risk. The card holder doesn't know exactly how the card particulars reach the merchant. The information could pass through multiple systems before it reaches its final destination. It would be possible for someone along the way to scan the card details and use the information illegally. This problem is being addressed by companies that have developed software that uses encryption. Encryption is a process that encodes details, such as the charge number, so that they can only be read by those who have the decoder.

Merchant Accounts — Processing credit cards requires a merchant account. Merchant accounts are not all the same. Credit card companies charge different fees to process accounts. These charges vary, so shop around.

The discount rate (the amount the credit card company will deduct from each charge they process) can range from 1.5% to 5%. Some will charge transactions fees or have monthly minimums that must be met. Generally, the more automated and computerized your transactions are, the lower your discount rate will be. The discount rate can be based on the average ticket price, usually going down as the ticket price goes up. Application and set up fees (often including software and hardware to process the charges) also vary and can easily go up to $1500, so these fees must be considered when making your decision to go with a specific card processor. Also, be sure and ask how soon the money will be deposited into your bank account. The deposit can be made within 24 hours or as long as seven days. Obviously, the quicker the better. If you apply for an American Express account in addition to Visa/MasterCard, American Express processing will usually take longer.

Your local bank can probably service your merchant account and will probably have reasonable rates. However, local banks are usually more conservative and will generally not process phone or Internet orders and may not allow as many privileges as national credit card companies. There is currently a bank, First Virtual Bank, that specializes in offering merchant accounts for Internet businesses. Most local banks require that the card be present and the consumer sign the charge slip, which would eliminate telephone orders or online transactions. The reason for this is that a telephone order doesn't have any proof that the cardholder authorized the purchase. Telephone orders have the highest return rates and the most disputed charges, so a local bank may deny your application if you intend to take primarily phone orders.

Applying for a merchant account and getting approval is a time-consuming process. Do not make the mistake of thinking you can start in business today and get a merchant account by next week. It doesn't happen. The credit card companies require extensive documentation of your financial stability, the reliability of your product, and customer service. One merchant claims the applications are approved based on the weight of the information supplied. ;) His formula for application is: include everything but the kitchen sink. Not every company requires the same information, but generally they ask for the following: product and advertising samples, financial statements on the principals of the company as well as the company itself.

Electronic Cash

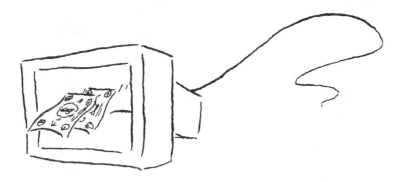

Electronic cash is the latest development toward conducting simple and safe monetary transactions over the Internet. It is a technology which works today. Several companies supply this service, and while specifics vary, the general approach is the same. To receive payments via e-mail, download the electronic cash software onto your computer. The software is generally compatible with most types of computers. The software links you to your bank and in turn to your potential clients. Your clients will not have to be linked to your electronic cash company to pay you. When the software is running, a toolbox will appear on the screen that contains icons or buttons that if clicked will help you make transactions with your bank and other e-cash users. Other clicked icons will show a current status report of your account. This e-cash software, depending on the developer, can be active in the background of your graphical browser program, such as Mosaic or Netscape (tools which allow you to move around the Net). If the e-cash software is active in the background, it will pop up when payment is required. This e-cash software makes it easy for consumers to purchase products quickly and easily. The software is also available for UNIX users.

Electronic Cash solves the big problem with monetary transactions over the Internet— the security issue. Before E-cash, computer hackers could capture all kinds of information that traveled over the network, including your credit card number, accounting information, and personal information. Another way to alleviate this problem is encryption, a process of coding information between a consumer and a vendor so that a transaction is confidential. Encryption is available on a limited basis, but like any new process it is expensive.

Section IV

Tools

The Internet has become easier to use with the advent of two popular graphical browsers Mosaic and Netscape. Nevertheless, doing business over the Internet still requires a knowledge of the tools necessary to work on the Net. Once you have this knowledge, mix it with a vision of the possibilities and your own creativity and skills. Willingness to think in new, imaginative ways is the key to success in making money on the Internet. Your business will quickly grow.

In the past, one of the drawbacks for a business was an inability to afford communication of sales information with the outside world. Advertising and sales are major requirements for success. Think of the people who have failed in business, despite great ideas, because they were unable to sell them. Those days are gone. With the Internet, communication with the whole world is possible for pennies. Well-written descriptions of your products and knowledge of the Internet tools are all you need to develop a clientele that you *know* is interested in your business. You can create a "virtual storefront" in cyberspace. You no longer need to go to the risk involved in leasing an actual facility. You don't need expensive, well-placed, and well-timed newspaper or magazine ads; any business can find success. You can now contact thousands, even millions, in a fraction of the time and at a fraction of the cost. Your virtual storefront will help people easily do business with you. Following are descriptions of the different tools you need to set up your store in cyberspace.

Chapter 19

World Wide Web

The World Wide Web (WWW, W3, or just the Web) is the hottest development in cyberspace. The growth on the Web is astounding with hundreds of new users obtaining a Web site every day. What is attracting all these new users? The Web is by far the most exciting and interesting Internet feature, and for many reasons it has the potential to become the best marketing tool available to businesses. The WWW

links thousands of servers, each containing a small portion of the Web's total information base. These servers are connected through a common, agreed upon protocol, which is HyperText Transfer Protocol (HTTP), the primary language of the Web. The program or interface which is used to explore the World Wide Web is called a browser. Three popular browsers are Mosaic, Netscape and Slipknot, which are available free on the Internet. Once you are connected to the Internet, download one of these programs, and you can easily access the World Wide Web.

In technical terms, the World Wide Web is officially described as a "wide-area hypermedia information retrieval initiative aiming to give universal access to a large universe of documents." Put simply, the WWW is a community of linked online information resources that appear in many different media forms. These online resources not only include businesses but also libraries, museums, service organizations, magazines, government records, resumés, and anything else imaginable. Commercial enterprises, however, are the fastest growing segment of the Web.

When using other tools of the Internet such as FTP, gopher, and telnet, Internet travelers can view only text. These data sites can contain pictures, sound, and images, but they cannot be viewed online. You don't ever visit gopher or FTP sites just because they are aesthetically pleasing — they are strictly utilitarian. Many thousands who cruise the Web daily do so to simply entertain themselves, because sightseeing on the World Wide Web is fun. Ingenuity is needed to draw consumers to a particular site. Creative color and graphics enhance Web pages, but they are not the only things attracting Web travelers.

Home Pages

The reason commercial entities are flocking to the World Wide Web is its incredible potential as a marketing medium. The Web's growing popularity stems from its ability to produce documents that contain a lot more than just text. Web users can incorporate color, sound, video, pictures, and graphics to create attractive and exciting documents on their Web sites. The Web also allows users to view documents quickly and easily. The number of people who reach and visit your Web site can far outnumber the people you reach by newspaper, TV, and magazine advertisements combined, and at a small fraction of the cost.

A business' Web "site" or address is also commonly referred to as a home page. A business uses a home page as an electronic store in cyberspace for all Internet travelers to see. Here a business can place its logo, information regarding its services and products, and anything else a business would like the world to know in a colorful and creative manner. The home page should then be linked to other areas, so Net users can visit it from many other sites. For suggestions of possible links, see Appendix 2: Places to Advertise on the Net.

HyperText Markup Language (HTML)

The Web is an interactive medium, meaning it is a participatory environment. This is another reason why people enjoy traveling the Web. Web travelers can participate in a variety of multimedia attractions including text, audio, video, color, pictures, and graphics. Interaction is made possible through hyperlinks. The various links are found on different Web pages. Linked access to home pages on the Web is specified by URLs (Universal Resource Locators) which are "addresses." These URLs indicate what the server is, where it is located, and where on that server the requested document is to be found.

To create a home page and access links you use HyperText Markup Language (HTML), a software language. HTML incorporates hyperlinks which enable you to link your home page to other areas at the click of a button. Home pages are fairly easy to create using software called HTML editors. It is not necessary to employ an HTML specialist to create your home page, but that service is certainly available if you don't want the bother. Some commercial sites on the Web will even create your home page as part of a package deal in setting up your site. See Appendix 2.

The key word in the HyperText Markup Language is hyper. If you add the prefix hyper to the words text, audio, video, and each of the other media, a Web page becomes a highly interactive and animated document. Collectively, these are called hypermedia. The first key to understanding how the Web works is to conceptualize what hypertext is and how it creates an actual Web of information.

In order to explain how hypertext works, let us imagine that we are cruising the Internet and that the page we are viewing is an actual WWW site devoted to NBA basketball. As we read, we notice that the names of several NBA teams are highlighted in a different color (sometimes underlined). You find that your favorite team is also highlighted. Curious about the highlighted words, you point your mouse, click on the highlighted name of your favorite team, and watch wide-eyed as the computer whisks you to a different document. You have discovered hypertext. Let us delve a little deeper into how to use hypertext.

If the text of an NBA Web site reads, "The <u>Utah</u>

Jazz is closing in on the NBA record for most consecutive road games won," you could click on the underlined or highlighted words Utah Jazz which is a hypertext link, and immediately you would be taken to a page devoted to the Utah Jazz. This page would probably contain information about the Jazz, their consecutive road game winning streak, and maybe a box score from their last game. The Utah Jazz page might also give information about an upcoming game with another team, say the San Antonio Spurs. If the Spurs' name is underlined or highlighted, this is another hypertext link and will lead to news and information about the Spurs.

At either site there might be a picture of Karl Malone dunking the basketball over Dennis Rodman. A sound could be linked to this picture so that when you clicked your mouse on it, the sound of shouting would roar from your speakers.

On the Spurs' page, there might also be a picture of David Robinson of the Spurs. You could click here and a biography, complete with pictures depicting aspects of the Admiral's career would appear on your screen. At the bottom you notice that the word Navy is highlighted in a paragraph about Robinson's college days at the Naval Academy. You decide to click on the word Navy. This link leads to the Naval Academy's Web site, which even contains recruiting information and a sign-up form. Hyperlinks can literally lead you on an endless adventure through cyberspace.

As you travel the Web, you will encounter not only words but a plethora of online graphics and some multimedia presentations. Anything that can be digitized, even video clips, can be incorporated into your home page. The Web will revolutionize the way products are sold and marketed. Some experts have compared the applications of the Web to the much hyped interactive television. They predict that one day the PC will replace television as the leading form of entertainment in the average household.

Businesses are taking advantage of the World Wide Web by creating interactive home pages that are linked to Web sites all over the world. Many businesses are finding that they can draw thousands of people to their home page by networking with other companies who do something related to their business. For example, if your company sells computer hardware, you might be able to convince IBM to place your company name in their home page as a hypertext link on the basis that you will sell truck loads of their computers. ;) Then all of the consumers that visit IBM's home page will have access to your home page because it is linked to IBM's home page. Needless to say, the marketing implications of the Internet and especially the World Wide Web are enormous.

Chapter 20

E-mail

   E-mail, electronic messages sent over computer networks, is currently the most widely used Internet tool. E-mail is being used by corporations in a variety of ways to help them conduct business. Many are using it to enhance their in-house communications. Companies find that e-mail saves time and money compared to traditional telephone and fax machine use. The only cost associated with e-mail is generally a flat monthly fee paid to an access provider for connecting to the Internet. There are no long distance

fees to pay, and best of all, you can avoid the delays and frustrations of telephone tag. E-mail lets you contact sales reps or customers, do research or collect data quickly and efficiently.

E-mail Addresses

E-mail addresses are usually numbers, letters, or a combination of both followed by an @ sign, followed by the domain name. They can be short or long. *Sidney Kramer Books,* for example, can be reached at **skbooks@clark.net.** On the other hand, *The Military Bulletin Board System* has this address: **afrespam@tecnet2.jcte.jcs.mil.** The important thing to remember is to type the address exactly as it appears, and you will be able to send a letter that will be received instantly.

Mail Lists

E-mail allows you to create electronic mailing lists or distribution lists that will transmit your sales letter or electronic brochure to hundreds of customers with just a few keystrokes on your computer. You can also subscribe to be on mailing lists through Listserv. This is where the Internet can be of tremendous value for the small business owner or independent entrepreneur. Because the cost of e-mail is negligible, his electronic brochure can compete with the big guy's.

Mailbots

A logical development in the use of e-mail to reach a wide audience is the mailbot. A mailbot can be set up to shoot answers back to potential customers automatically. The mailbot can deliver the most recent information in a matter of minutes, 24 hours a day, all year round. In an age when fast responses can really make the difference in a sale, a mailbot makes a lot of sense. Since the majority of Internet users have e-mail access, and sometimes only that, your target audience can include virtually everyone on the Net. When a potential customer contacts your mailbot via e-mail, the 'bot sends your prepared document, news or sales letter back to the writer. You have a built-in, self-selected target market of those people who contacted your 'bot.

The 'bot also gathers some very valuable information for you. It collects the names and e-mail addresses of those who contact it. This service provides you with the beginning of a database of potential clients. You can then follow up with further communication. Your 'bot can also log the activity of your account, both the times and amounts. This data helps you in your test marketing, because you can tell right away what sort of copy, information, or newsletter pulls in the responses, where your customers live, and how they discovered your site.

And you can make changes quickly to any aspect of your automated responses/advertisements in order to improve performance. You can also restrict who has access to your 'bot by creating a password system for authorized users. If you want to have multiple accounts so that you can track which advertisements are the most successful, you can create alias accounts. Think of the marketing power of a World Wide Web site **and** the enhanced instant communication capabilities of a mailbot.

Listservs

Another easy way to amplify business-related communication is to set up a listserv. Listservs are an extension of e-mail, but the messages are not sent one-to-one. Instead, one message is sent to a list of many people at one time. In-house communication using a listserv would work this way. A company has a mailing list of all those people who periodically need to be contacted, for whatever reason, to fix bugs, advertise a new product, update price and inventory lists, etc. When an announcement needs to be made, a message would be sent by e-mail to everyone on the list. Obviously this method of communication is much faster and easier for the sender, but it is also more convenient for the receiver, who can read his e-mail at his ease.

A listserv can also be used to send newsletters to customers. Roswell James owns a bookstore in remote Nova Scotia, but his location doesn't stop him from reaching a worldwide market on the Internet. Roswell explains that everything in his business has improved since he has gone on the Net. His entire store sales have doubled over the previous year's sales. The only thing that he did differently was that he set up his store on the World Wide Web (**http://www.nstn.ca**) and gopher (**gopher.nstn.ca**). Every day he finds e-mail orders coming in over the Internet. He describes it as "just incredible." These orders come in from every part of the world including Europe, Australia, Japan, and many different parts of the United States. It has opened up the world to him, and he is part of the global village. Mr. James keeps a database of customers from every country in the world, and once a month it takes him about twenty minutes to transmit a four-page newsletter of new releases with specials of the month with his listserv. "This is very serious advertising, and it only cost about 65 cents . . . total . . . to be in communication with about 450 customers."

If the list owner does not wish to initiate the use of the list, he can post files that interested members may download as they desire. Help files and archives of discussions that may be useful to clients can also be made available with listserv. Listservs are also valuable to businesses or entrepreneurs who are interested in discussing issues and problems related to business, or who are looking for mentors or contacts. It works this way. A person poses a problem or topic for discussion to the list. Then other list members post their replies, offer help or advice, or share their expertise. The posts, those messages and replies sent to the list, are e-mailed to everyone on the list. Each member then chooses which messages to read. Some topics may be vitally interesting to a member. Others can be quickly deleted. You join a listserv by sending an e-mail message to the list owner. Usually you provide your name, e-mail address, business, and the words **Subscribe <listname>-L**.

Some newcomers to Internet listservs have been confused about the procedure for "unsubscribing" to a list. Perhaps the confusion lies in the similarity between listservs and newsgroups. To unsubscribe from a newsgroup, you do indeed click on "unsubscribe." The procedure is different for a listserv, and the necessary words vary from list to list. Usually you send an e-mail message to the owner of the list with a short message such as **signoff <listname>-L**. It may help you to remember the difference if you think: "I 'unsubscribe' to newsgroups and 'signoff' from listservs." Be certain to get a copy of the FAQs (Frequently Asked Questions) when you first join the list so that you'll know the procedure they want you to use to sign off.

One of the disadvantages of a listserv is that a very active group can inundate you with list mail which fills up lots of disk space. Good listservs, however, are worth the few minutes it takes you to electronically sort through your mail. See Appendix 3: Business and Business Related Listservs, where we have included some listservs which are devoted to business and business-related topics.

Some customer-oriented companies have set up discussion groups on the Internet strictly for their customers to voice concerns and have those concerns resolved. This can be compared to a real-time newsletter devoted to customer wants, needs, and concerns. What a great way to improve a business' most valuable resource--its customers! Direct marketing will truly become the personalized marketing tool it was intended to become.

Chapter 21

Gopher

Gopher is the aptly-named menu searcher of cyberspace. It is a searching tool that digs through volumes of information to find just exactly what you want. Gopher searches from general menus to increasingly more specific ones. It brings up a menu and allows you to progress menu by menu. The search becomes more specific with each menu, until you reach your destination. There are no fancy graphics to click on, but you can still get where you want to go rather easily. Menus are linked by text only. An example would be a book search at your local library where the first screen gives you a choice of type of search (author, subject, title) and after you make your selection, another menu appears on your screen. You then make additional selections until the description, location, and status of the book are before you.

Gopher works the same way on the Internet. You make choices from menus until the final product or article appears on the screen. For an excellent example of the use of gopher, check out the Seaside Book & Stamp Co. in Halifax, Nova Scotia, Canada **(gopher://cyberservices.nstn.ca:70/11/e-mall/**

Bookstore/seaside). Gopher is set up here to help customers search first by category (mystery, science fiction, fantasy, adventure, etc.) and then by author. Each entry is well-supported with information about the price of the book, how to order it, and a form for doing so.

Gopher is also valuable for various business tasks. It can be used to do copyright and trademark searches. It can help you discover local job listings. It can provide you with travel information on possible problems in unstable areas. At least one journalist uses it to get story leads. The National Science Foundation keeps an archive of abstracts on research projects. Keyword searches can lead to interesting articles on current or past projects. The journalist uses gopher to find articles and then contacts the writer directly for interviews or further information on late-breaking developments.

Another mouth-watering example of gopher is found at the Fine Food Emporium site **(gopher://garnet.msen/com:70/00/vendor/emporium/gourmet.food.catalog**). There are no pictures at this site, of course, but the text descriptions of their gourmet food products are enough to make you drool and order. They include prices in addition to their Web site and e-mail addresses. Their gopher site demonstrates that it's not necessary to have fancy graphics and hyperlinks to produce a compelling business page. A good copywriter can make all the difference in creating a successful gopher site.

Most businesses would benefit from having both a World Wide Web site and a gopher site. The gopher site offers the same information as the home page, but it's all in text form. Although it is possible to transmit graphics, sound and video clips to your gopher customers, they cannot be seen or heard online. These things can be downloaded and then viewed off line. Of course, gopher is not as attractive as a World Wide Web home page, but many people who are currently online don't yet have the capability of accessing Web sites. You wouldn't want to miss a very large target market by ignoring the possibility of a gopher site, even if the only thing these potential customers can see online is text. An example of an interesting application of gopher is at the gopher site for the rock band *live* **(gopher mediafive.yyz.com)**. The band's site leads to a discography, transcriptions of interviews, back issues of e-mailing list digests, tour information, and song lyrics.

Many Internet travelers use the Net to gather information in order to make a decision about a purchase they make in the traditional ways. For this reason alone, a gopher site can be very valuable to a business. Electronic files can be accessed by interested buyers who choose the kind of information they desire. These files can contain such diverse information as product description, clipped articles about the business and/or the product, lists of locations where the product is found, seminar dates and registration information, customer feedback, success stories, biographies of the developer, and excerpts of articles or books that will entice the reader to know more. Use of gopher in this manner is a good way to boost sales and credibility. Whether the sale is made over the Internet or in the local store, it's still a sale, and gopher can be another valuable tool in your package of marketing strategies.

gopher

To set up a gopher site:

1. Register free with the Mother of all Gophers at the University of Minnesota by sending an e-mail request to **gopher@boombox.micro.umn.edu**.

2. Get a software program. This is often supplied through your local access provider. It's also available on the Internet as freeware. Check **gopher:// hopf.math.nwu.edu:70/11/** or **ftp.acns.nwu.edu** and get the file in the subdirectory **pub/gn/gn/tar.gz**. This is a multi-protocol server which means that it will support both gopher and HyperText Transfer Protocol (HTTP) which is the protocol you need for the Web.

3. Register your gopher business site online with places such as **gopher://garnet.msen.com:70/1** or **gopher://product.com**. The registration may be free, or there may be a small monthly fee.

Chapter 22

FTP

With all the excitement of graphical browsers like Mosaic, Netscape, and Slipknot, why would you want to use FTP, the workhorse of the Internet? FTP, which stands for File Transfer Protocol, is really the

backbone of the Net and is its most widely used feature. It allows you to take yourself in a figurative way to another computer's files, literally get what you need, and store it in your own computer's files, all without leaving your home or office. Each day thousands of hosts are transferring countless files all over the world from one computer to another. It only takes a few minutes, and it's free! The reason this can be done is one of the miracles of the present age and certainly the main cause of the technological revolution that is spreading throughout the world. In a singularly unique spirit of cooperation, certain conventions called protocols were developed so that all computers could "talk" to each other and be able to quickly pass on critical Defense department information. This cooperation then extended to the academic and scientific communities in order to share vital research files. This is why the Internet works. People can communicate in a global community because the developers of the system 25 years ago were able to agree on certain conventions, and through the years they have continued to do so. This is why the world knows about attempted coups in Moscow and Port-au-Prince, earthquake survivors in California and Japan, and war in the Persian Gulf *while* these events are happening. Anyone who has dealt with any sort of bureaucracy can appreciate this miracle of cooperation.

So how can FTP be valuable to you in the business world? FTP can help you find and disseminate mountains of information. With all this information available, will the *selling* of information become obsolete? Absolutely not. There is so much information out there, and most of us see only our own tiny little corner. Anyone that organizes a well-written and well-developed electronic newsletter or article will be appreciated by those customers who don't have the time to do that kind of research or who would be more effective using their time on other projects.

Business can benefit from using FTP in at least four ways. First of all, even though there are more than 30 million people accessing the Internet, at least a third of them don't have full Internet access. They are only able to use e-mail, gopher, and FTP. That's a potential target market of 10 million people, so you'll probably want to consider having an FTP site. Secondly, FTP is probably the quickest way to retrieve files on the Internet. You'll remember that gopher is a good method for finding something when you know where to go, but not exactly what you want. It takes you through a series of menus until you arrive at your destination. Even without the possibility of viewing graphics or having sound clips online, gopher is a fairly good way to find certain types of information. When using FTP, you can't view *anything* online, all you see on the screen are the names of file directories of the host computer. You have to know ahead of time exactly what you are after, the name of the directory where it is located, and the name of the file itself. You need to know exactly what you want and where it is.

FTP isn't really used for browsing. When you find the files you want to bring to your computer, you download them first, then read them later offline. This could be a real money saver to your business. Keep a list of valuable FTP sites and keep it updated by consulting the trade magazines (such as *NetGuide* or *NetWorld*) or the lists available on the Internet itself. See Appendix 4: FTP Sites for some ideas on beginning your FTP list. Check the sites on your list often, and you will quickly know when new software is released or where to find the improved versions of shareware. This kind of "sharing" can greatly reduce your business costs. You can have the files "transported" to your computer within minutes. This sort of speed is essential for remaining on the cutting edge.

An FTP site can also help you with secondary marketing as well as provide the capability of giving excellent customer support. You can keep files at your site concerning product improvements, price lists, sales literature, order forms, gifts, catalogs, a few chapters of a book, sound and video clips, and Frequently Asked Questions (FAQs) about your product. These sorts of files help you give technical support at any time 24 hours a day.

Another advantage of an FTP site is that you can capture the e-mail addresses of all those who log on.

Typically the user goes to your site and logs on as "anonymous." Then the user is asked for a password, which is usually his e-mail address. This means that all of those potential customers who have come to your site have left calling cards. You have a built-in electronic mailing list of people who have already expressed interest in your product. You can follow up with sales letters that can be sent and received in just minutes for pennies. So not only do you have a preselected mailing list, you also have the advantage of being able to communicate with potential prospects while they are most interested. Instead of days and weeks passing by as would be the case with snail mail, you can follow up and close the sale right away. Time no longer works against you.

When you use FTP, you have to know the location of the file and its name. There are no organized menus or hypertext links to help you move from one place to another. When using gopher, you jump from one menu to another menu until you reach the right file. These menus may or may not be in close proximity. FTP enables you to make the first big jump to the site, then poke around in the files that are located there. Does that mean that you can go to any company's files and look at whatever you want? Or that anyone with a computer and an Internet connection can go through all of your business documents? No. Companies typically keep their downloadable files in a subdirectory called */pub* for public. That means that anonymous logins (browsers) are free to look at and access only the public files, but they will be denied access to all other company files. Other companies with FTP sites do not allow anonymous logins. This means all users must be authorized and registered with the company in order to gain access to their files.

What if you only have access to e-mail? Can you still take advantage of FTP? Most emphatically yes! You can e-mail your requests for files to any computer that acts as an FTP mail server (such as FTP mail@decwrl.dec.com). Of course you'll have to know where the file is and what its name is, but the requested file can be mailed back to you by e-mail in a few minutes or the next day.

With FTP you can download unlimited information and software such as Web browsers, newsreaders, etc. Let's look at the way FTP works. Naturally you must have the appropriate program, an FTP client. This is usually part of the package supplied by your local access provider. Enter the program and a screen will appear that asks for an FTP address. For this example, let's find the Web browser, Netscape. In the host name line, type the address, **ftp.mcom.com**. Next, you need to enter your e-mail address. Do this by putting a check in the anonymous login box, and your e-mail address will automatically be inserted. Click the "Save Configuration" button because you may want to visit this site again. Click the "OK" button. For the next few seconds you will see messages flash across the screen as your computer talks to the computer at the host site.

When your access is confirmed, a screen will appear which is basically divided into quadrants. The quadrants on the left side tell information about *your* computer, and the quadrants on the right side tell information about the *remote host* computer. On the left side, indicate where you want to store the *Netscape* files that will be downloaded. On the right side you see a list of directories on the top. Double-click on *Netscape*. In the same square, there will now be three choices: "Mac, UNIX, and Windows." Mark the appropriate choice. In the bottom screen, the names of the files that you can access will appear. Mark the files you want, and double click on the left arrow in the middle of the screen. In a few minutes you will see that these files have been transferred to your computer because they will now be listed on the left side of the screen. Close the connection, exit from your Internet connection, and read the files from the directory where you saved them. That's all there is to it!

Be polite. It is a good idea to do your downloading after business hours. During the day some companies will deny you access completely because they need their computers to do their business tasks. You will probably find it easier and quicker to login to remote computers if you do so after the close of *their* business day.

Chapter 23

Usenet

The Usenet newsgroups or discussion groups are similar to the bulletin boards at the local supermarket. Anyone can post a message for all to see. Usenet newsgroups use the Internet to make their bulletin board format available to interested readers throughout the world. Like the Listservs, the newsgroups have one-to-many communication, but it is not e-mail based, instead it is accessed through a newsreader program. Newsreader software is available through your access provider, or it's free over the Internet. Imagine a large bulletin board where someone has posted a topic for discussion such as motorcycles. Anyone in the world who wants to talk about motorcycles can subscribe to this discussion group by looking at his provider's list of available newsgroups (there are more than 10,000 of them) and clicking on the name of the group. Subscribing means that you have added a group to your list for your newsreader interface to manage. You don't go through any subscription process or pay any fees; you just register. Anyone who has subscribed to the group can post messages on the electronic bulletin board. The messages are posted on the local server which then routes them all over the world to other servers. Then anyone who wants to read the notices can subscribe to the group and read them. When you don't want to read the group's messages anymore, you simply unsubscribe.

There are discussion groups for just about any topic that you can imagine. They are usually divided into hierarchies such as:

comp -	computer related topics
news -	topics relating to the newsgroups, announcements of newsgroups
rec -	games, arts, pets, Star Trek, music, sports, hobbies
sci -	science related topics
soc -	social interactions, various cultures, history, politics, religion, feminism, roots
talk -	hot topics for discussion, archived discussions, largely debate-oriented
alt -	subjects of a personal nature or current issues.
bionet -	topics for biologists
biz -	business related topics
bit -	redistribution of Bitnet

In addition, there are other specialized lists, some of which may require a subscription fee, but the categories listed above are the most commonly used.

Going back to our motorcycle topic, suppose that we want to discuss dirt bikes. In our list of newsgroups, there is one named *rec.motorcycles.dirt*. That's the one that we most likely would want. While looking at the list, we see that there are several other groups that discuss motorcycles (*rec.motorcycles.harley* and *rec.motorcycles.racing*), and we decide to subscribe to these also. After a quick look at *the .harley* group, it does not appear to qualify. We decide to unsubscribe to that one, but we'll keep the others. Our newsreader program keeps track of all the decisions we have made.

With literally millions of users accessing the Usenet newsgroups every day, the advantages to the business community seem obvious. Why not simply compose an ad for your product and post it to every newsgroup on the Internet? This is known as "spamming" and should be avoided for historical as well as practical reasons. Usenet was started in 1979 as an experiment to connect two universities in North Carolina. Other academic sites were connected during the 80's and 90's, and now there are more than three million users and almost a million sites. Although no one manages the Net, there are a certain number of conventions which became accepted over the years. At first, absolutely no advertising was allowed. The Internet was expected to be used only for research and educational purposes. Now there are certain places where advertising is tolerated and even expected, but no one knows for sure how the commercialization of the Net will affect the newsgroups. If you plan to advertise in the newsgroups, look for the appropriate places, like the *misc.forsale* and the *biz* groups. These groups are some of the most popular newsgroups, so there are many potential customers out there in cyberspace, and they aren't hostile to advertising. In fact, they welcome it.

Another practical reason to avoid "spamming" is the impossibility of fulfillment. How are you going to get your product to 30 million people, or even one million, or even 50 thousand? Do you have the resources and the inventory to meet the demand? These are things to consider before posting messages to newsgroups. It is best to start with a rather small test market and see how you do, before you launch into a full scale Internet campaign. Your company's reputation is on the line, and you will want to be able to process orders efficiently and quickly, offering impeccable service and customer support.

Some newsgroups absolutely do not want any sort of advertising. Users are not shy about expressing their opinions if you try to disregard their conventions, and you may be "flamed," a particularly vicious form of verbal attack which consists of electronic hate mail. It is easy to find out about the conventions or desires

of a particular newsgroup. Most newsgroups have a
list of FAQs, which will tell you what they allow and
what conditions they attach to use. Of course the
misc.forsale groups are about selling as well as the
biz.marketplace and *biz.misc* ones. Legitimate
postings to other groups should be on-topic, hype-free,
short and relevant, and perhaps point the reader to your
WWW page or the *biz.misc.* area. If you decide to
ignore the newsgroups' conventions, be prepared for
the consequences. Can you or your company afford
the backlash and the damaged reputation? Only you
can decide if the risk is worth it.

Chapter 24

BBSs and Online Commercial Services

If you have an account with GEnie, Prodigy, or CompuServe, are you already on the Internet? Yes, and no. The big commercial services like these listed give you limited access to the Internet. They choose which features of the Internet they wish to carry. They then organize the features in an easy-to-use format for their customers. The keyword here is *limited*; currently you cannot access every Net feature through

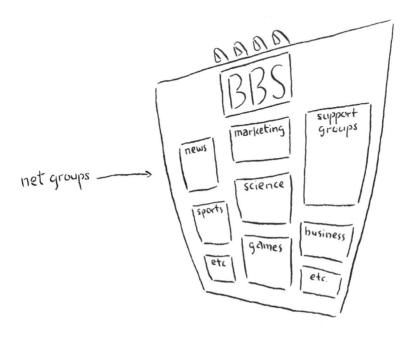

the commercial services. Their access is expanding, and in the future, users will no doubt demand full Internet access from these gateways, but it is not available now. Another key phrase is *easy-to-use*. The Internet is so dynamic and so vast that it can sometimes be daunting to venture forth into cyberspace. The commercial online services make it easier, and they provide technical support.

Such big commercial services are actually nationwide bulletin board systems or BBSs. There are hundreds of local BBSs throughout the world. Most of them are in North America, but there are also some in Japan, Europe, and South Africa. These local BBSs can be accessed by telnet or modem. After you have registered with them, you usually pay an hourly fee for connect time. Registration consists of giving the system operator, or sysop, your real name, address, telephone number, birth date and sex. You choose a nickname and a password. Most of the time you are allowed limited access; this access is really just a little teaser to enable you to see what sort of features they have. Later, usually within the next 24 hours, the sysop will do a voice verification (that's why they need your telephone number). After that you can send in other paper verification and payment if required. Other BBSs will let you charge your time over the modem with your Visa or MasterCard.

The local BBSs like to think of themselves as "entertainment social systems." Many of them have interesting names like Canned Ham, Alien's SpaceShip, Barney's Rubble, and one of the most fascinating - FlOaTIng PancReAs. They often give you access to the Internet (for an additional fee), but they also have scads of fun features that thousands access every day. On the BBSs you can find shareware, clip art, pictures, sounds, weather maps and forecasts, private and local chat, IRC chat and worldlink, sports connections, stocks, tv listings, movie reviews, the Daily News feed, tourism info, humor, demos, music, programming support files, matchmakers, and games.

Games are a hot item on the BBSs. People from all over the world play games with each other in real time. Some of the most popular are Trade Wars, Mutants, Blade Master, Galactic Empire, Shadow Realms, and Fantasy Football. You can role play globally with people who have similar interests.

Some bulletin boards are geared to specific audiences. There are several software developers who have established their own bulletin boards to test and market their software. It's an easy way to provide product improvements, updates, and debugging programs. *Bryant.com,* for instance, manufactures, demonstrates, and resells software with entertainment and utility applications for other BBSs. These are available to registered users only. *Elysian Fields* has computer components from Galacticomm and related distributors. They also help customers join the Internet system.

Other BBSs cater to ham radio enthusiasts, appraisers (one BBS has an online database that is an invaluable resource for appraisers and investors), country music fans, those interested in conferencing on environmental or health issues, supporters of the arts, alternative education or politics. The bulletin board called *The Pressroom*, for example, has press schedules and transcripts, local forums on media issues, and keyword searches of White House documents. With *Online Orlando*, on the other hand, you can get feedback from WJRR radio station disk jockeys and access a 15,000 piece lyric library. Station 540AM has a 24-hour sports station. *Online Orlando* also carries trivia games such as Trek Trivia and online role playing.

Bulletin Boards can be a valuable tool for businesses if you are targeting a local audience, have a high need for security, or if you want to have a customized board. *The Doctor's Office BB* has all the usual fun and games plus a 24-hour link to *The Doctor's Clinic BB* in Manassas, VA.

DataCom carries a PC online catalog so that you can comparison shop for computer hardware and software. If you have a very specialized product, or if you are dealing in software, you might want to create your own bulletin board. Even though they are a lot of work to maintain, your security needs may balance that out. *The Flower Link* has its own bulletin board. Since there is a lot of online courting going on (see *Christie's Internet Matchmaker BB*), an online floral company has a lot of sales appeal. Same day flower delivery is a great moneymaker.

If you don't need your own bulletin board, you might want to consider some of the BBSs that have online shopping as well as other fun features. Consider your target market. If your product appeals to males who are under thirty, the bulletin boards are a good place to market your product. You'll want to visit *Magnus Online*, where each user is entitled to one free WWW or gopher page. You can also make your files available for FTP. See Appendix 5: Bulletin Board Systems for other business BBSs. These are the ones that currently accept advertising.

Section V

Business Ideas for the Internet — Spark Your Imagination

Are you looking for a business idea to take on the Internet? Let the following ideas spark your imagination. Read through them, keeping your own unique skills and talents in mind. Then use your creativity to establish your place in this new technological world. The ideas are divided into eight categories. The categories are not rigid and ideas should be able to float between the divisions. The categories were established in an effort to help people who have identified different personal skills and strengths to move quickly into those areas where they will experience the greatest success. For instance, if you know you have marketing skills, you can concentrate your efforts in a marketing business. Read through all the ideas however, because you may spot a "service idea" that you could market successfully.

Chapter 25

Business

For the purpose of this list, the following are ideas for businesses which require some skill or training. Obviously, because of the training involved, not every idea will work for everyone, but the ideas are presented as an catalyst for creativity. These hints should help you generate ideas of how you can utilize your talents and skills in the Net market. For example, you would be amazed at the number of companies and professions, from lawyers to day care services, that hate to bill and do a lousy job at it. Half the time they don't follow right up with a second reminder, and it goes downhill from there. If you have accounting or business skills, you can offer to do the billing or accounting for these professionals. Start small. Find one business (doctor, plumber, pre-school, etc.) and give them a deal to get your foot in the door and gain experience. Use the Internet as a communication vehicle so they have instant access to you. Do a good job and as your business builds, you can begin to advertise over the Net!

Tax preparation is another useful business service. It is somewhat seasonal, but if tax season is during the "slow" time of the year for your business, it could be a good way to make a little extra money. H & R Block and other commercial tax preparation services hold classes in the fall to train people as employees. Attend one of the classes, work for them for one tax season, and then start your own business. Community colleges and high school continuing education programs also have classes in tax preparation. Learn the ropes in one of these classes, then with one of the many tax preparation programs available for free on the Net, you can establish your own tax preparation business and advertise your services over the Net. Check relevant World Wide Web sites for information that will keep you current on the tax law and for federal income tax forms that you can download and print. The IRS even has its own home page and you'll have access to documents and instructions. Your client's location is irrelevant because you can transmit the data back and forth electronically. See Appendix 6: Sites Related to Tax Issues.

If you possess great research skills, find a way to utilize this talent. For instance, finding family roots is one of the world's most popular hobbies. If you have an interest in genealogy, you can use your Internet connection to gain access to discussion groups and research archives devoted to genealogy. These Net resources will allow you to conduct and compile records for others. People searching out their roots make the Genealogy Bulletin Board one of the most popular sites on the Net. If you have access to genealogical, census, birth, marriage, or death records, you could locate information for your clients. Many people are more than willing to pay someone to organize the information that they have collected about their ancestors. You might have expertise in a certain area or language that would be of value. Mention your services in the appropriate newsgroups such as the *soc.genealogy* or *soc.culture* groups. Of course there is a lot of exchange of free information in these groups; that is a good thing. People researching the same lines are more than willing to share their information. You would not be competing with that. Original research specialists charge anywhere from $10 to $25 an hour. Several programs exist that will get you started. The most popular genealogy computer program is offered for less than $50 by The Church of Jesus Christ of Latter-Day Saints (Mormons). Other helpful programs are available as shareware over the Net.

Handouts, business cards, and wedding announcements are popular items that require someone with artistic typesetting skills. Form a good relationship with a printer and hang out your shingle on the Net. Your client can view your ideas online, through e-mail, or even by fax. Charge for your typesetting service and then a little extra for lining up the printer. As you begin to make money, the printer should also refer business to you. A relationship with a photographer is also important. Stay on the cutting edge. Subscribe to a graphics or typesetting newsgroup to keep current on new ideas. One idea that hasn't hit the magazines yet is thermographic paper which changes color with temperature. When you touch a thermographic business card, it will change colors—say from red to yellow. That catches people's attention. At least two companies in the United States will supply color-change paper to you for your clients. The paper is expensive, but well worth it.

OK, so you don't have accounting or research skills. Look through the list. Do any of these ideas appeal to you? Review your background. Read Internet discussion group messages in areas that interest you. You may discover abilities and skills that you had not realized would be so valuable. Use your imagination! Here are just a few ideas:

Accounting
Advertising Layout
Audits
Billing and Invoicing
Business Plans
Career Planning
Claims Processing
Clothes Design

Cost Estimating
Credit Agency
Data Entry
Debugging
Electronic Circuitry Design
Energy Consultant
Fashion Merchandising
Genealogy Extraction
Hobby Supplies
Home Builder's Kit
Home Improvement Designs
Jewelry Design
Job Placement and Referral
Legal Papers
Private Investigation
Tax Consultant/Preparer
Typesetting
Video Editing

Chapter 26

 **Education**

If you would like to work in education, there are many untapped areas that you can explore to form a business on the Internet. There are the traditional tutoring and manual writing opportunities. Here you share your skills and talents by training others. The training can take place either in person or through a medium such as books, cassettes or videos, but have you considered that online training is also possible through the use of IRC (Internet Relay Chat)? You could use your Internet connection to "occupy a room" and be available to answer questions, give useful information, and hear feedback from your clients. Specific and detailed answers could be sent by e-mail with or without an attached file that you have prepared off line. If you have a lot of business, and we hope you do, you can even set up a mail robot which will answer standard questions called FAQs (Frequently Asked Questions) or send out your information packet automatically. FAQs can also be available to be downloaded by current and potential customers at your Web site. Concentrate on a unique way to market your services over the Internet.

Don't think, however, that these traditional areas are the only opportunities. Education doesn't have to necessarily involve teaching. For instance, you could form a needs-resource matching business. A good example would be in the area of scholarships. Millions of scholarship dollars are unclaimed each year. Believe it or not, applicants just don't know about the scholarships, so they never apply. Several companies have databases to match applicants' qualifications with the available scholarships, grants, or awards requiring those qualifications. The databases are large! Usually, a company maintains the database, and you just transmit the information on a client to the search company which then does the search. It should only cost you $15- $45 to have the search done, once you have established a relationship with the search company. Although at least one company has given the scholarship search programs a bad name, the service is valid, and for a very low start-up cost (several hundred dollars), you can set yourself up in the scholarship searching business. Use your computer in this business to track your own clients. You'll have an edge because you can get the information to them *fast*. Students sometimes let deadlines creep up on them and lose out on scholarship opportunities. If you can provide rush searches, and you can if you communicate over the Internet, you'll have a most sought-after business.

Consider ways to help your local schools. Set up a business that arranges fund-raisers for schools. Vice-president Gore has told us that one goal of the present administration is to have every school and library in the country hooked up to the Internet by the year 2000. Interactive learning programs complete with graphics and sound will be in great demand throughout the country. At the present time, children can "visit" the Exploratorium in San Francisco, take a "picture tour" through the Louvre in Paris, or "discover" the treasure of the Smithsonian in Washington without leaving home. Students will be learning at their own pace as they access math, science, or history programs. You could have a part in developing the next generation of problem solvers. Think of your areas of interest. Could you plan an interactive program for the computer which would teach students how to care for the planet or how to write short stories? Every field of education will need new ideas on how to teach students using the latest computer technology. You don't need to know how to write the computer program yourself; you can hire your local computer guru to do that. All you need is a good idea. Read the following list for these and other education ideas.

Abstracter
Academic Tutoring
Aptitude Testing
Article Generation
Book Lists

CD-Rom Reference
Computer Customized Education Materials
Computer Design
Computer Interactive Education Materials
Computer Tutoring
Computer Seminars
Diet Advice Newsletter
Diet Menu Planner
Disk Tutoring Programs
Fund-raising
Information Research
Internet Training
Language Learning Software
Legal Papers
Manual Writing
Music Teacher Methods
Research
Resumé Preparation Advice
Retirement Planning
Scholarship Matching Service
Software Manuals
Software Programming
Speed Reading
Study Abroad Database
Support Groups
Test Scoring
Testing (all sorts)
Typing Tutor
Word Processing Classes

Chapter 27

Management

You would be amazed at the number of different businesses which require management help. Some of them are aware of this need, while others don't even know they need help. Think of the potential profits you can make and the service you will give if you make these businesses aware of this problem. For example, most businesses never contact their clients again once the client has dealt with them. Big mistake! A client who has already dealt with the business is the most important asset the business has. Why not keep all the client information on a computer database and "nurse" the clients along for a second sale? Have a clerk or secretary at the store or business take the names, addresses, phone numbers and other information about the clients. Enter the clients' information into the computer. This information can be sent to you electronically by e-mail or modem, and then you can help maintain a good relationship between business and customer. Once you have all of the clients' information, send them thank you notes. Tell them about new products or services in a letter, or send out advertising. Consider sending the clients a company newsletter. Offer to coordinate the company's bill payments, handle client billing, or keep track of client services required. Your service will help the company grow.

Don't be content with just managing clients. Many companies need help managing their inventory, personnel, or budgets. Find creative ways to help companies in these areas, and your services will be invaluable. Fulfilling these services over the Net will be lightening quick. Speed is often the bottom line in today's hectic corporate world. Many company executives, for example, are required to make presentations where they need special charts, graphs, handouts, or overhead slides. The company may lack the skilled personnel, the equipment, or the time to generate these presentation materials. There are commercial preparation services that will generate these materials, but they are very expensive. Without any overhead except your computer, you should be able to do a nice job preparing the needed materials if you know a graphics program inside and out. The presentations can be done in color, and they look great. No, you don't need a color printer. Local copy shops have color printers, and they will print your work for a minor charge. Graphs, charts, and even pictures can be transmitted to customers electronically.

Another way to supply management help is to contact property owners and offer to manage their property. Many of the pains of property ownership can be alleviated, or at least the pain can be reduced, by using computer programs which organize all of the functions associated with being a landlord. Many people like to own real estate, but hate to manage it, and they are willing to pay someone with a computer to keep track of all of the loose ends. (You could also offer to run utility audits for real estate owners. See ideas below on energy consultation.)

Here is a list of management ideas. Why not accept the challenge to think of other ways to render management services?

Bar Coding Services
Budgeting
Cash Flow Tracking
Client Tracking and Management
Data Management
Delivery Routes
Equipment Management
Inventory Control
Mail List Management
Manage Medical Billing, Invoicing, etc.
Mortgage Reduction Service
Newspaper Routes
Presentation Support
Property Management
Small Business Management Package
Tickler Systems
Web Site Set-up and Maintenance

Chapter 28

 Marketing

If you become skilled in marketing, you will "hold the world by its tail." No business can succeed without marketing, and companies will pay plenty for a successful marketing campaign. Let's face it, no matter how good a product is, unless you know how to get it to the market, it is of no value. Now is the time to learn what it takes to market on the Information Superhighway. Until now, marketing and advertising have been expensive. The basis of marketing is to reach as many people as possible, and this has been very costly. The Net is an inexpensive way to discover markets. Check out the literally thousands of different newsgroups. There are groups devoted to Star Trek, pets, investments, travel, business opportunities, sports, food, software, and games. There are thousands of interests out there. Find out what people are talking about and wish they had or wish they knew. Create a pamphlet or develop a specialized product that will be of help to those people, and you have a built-in market. Compared to traditional markets, it is not too costly to get a computer and modem and perfect your marketing skills on the Net. When you have those skills mastered, the world will literally beat a path to your door. You could also hire a computer guru to write your ads, answer inquiries and send out your catalogs or brochures by e-mail and use your time in product development, writing, or customer service. No matter which way you use the advantages of computer technology, you will benefit.

OK, what should you market? Well, what are your skills? If you are artistic and run a computer, for instance, consider becoming a graphic designer. Establish a relationship with a printer. There are lots of businesses that need their order forms designed or redesigned. Lots of stores use standard forms and sales receipts. If a printer will work with you (there are lots of printers looking for work, so you shouldn't have a problem finding one), you can give a store a custom form for a great price. That will help the store, the printer, and you can make money too. It is a win-win-win situation.

Do you have a hobby or unique interest that others would like to learn? Do you throw "great" parties? Do you have a one-of-a-kind product? One woman gives kitchen parties where she lets her guests try the utensils and new recipes before they buy. She can reach suppliers and obtain out-of-the-ordinary items over the Internet. You can sell just about anything on the Net from information to hobby supplies, antiques, and office equipment. Consider the following list, or make up your own.

Astrology Advice
Antique Value Advice
Baseball Cards
Birthday Party Package
Calendar of Events
Computer Art
Computer Customizing
Customized Forms
Creative Writing
Dating Idea Service
Design and Market Cross Stitch Patterns
Design and Market Cards, Labels, Banners, etc.
Direct Mail Marketing
Distressed Merchandise
Electronic Ad Service
Electronic Clip Art
Electronic Horoscope
Electronic Music (create and market)
Follow-up Marketing
Graphic Design
Kitchen Parties
List Brokering
Managing Stocks
Medical Billing
Newspaper Routes
Net Publishing
Party Idea Package
Personal Record Creation, Organization
Phone Consultant
Pogs

Property Management
Reunion Planning
Sales Assistance
Shopping Services
Special Occasion Announcements
Wholesale Sources
Wedding Planner

Chapter 29

Needs-Resource Matching

If you see a need, fill it. Computers are used in numerous fields to make a needs-resource match. For example, Dr. Norm Brown in Seattle matches companies looking for new technologies with the inventors of new technologies. His clients are actually large companies, universities, and the biggest is the Federal government. He doesn't need to spend the time and the money to travel to his clients' locations because the data can be transmitted over the Internet in just minutes. He can develop an international clientele without the constraints of time and distance. Can you think of sellers, buyers, or renters that could be matched? Cars (you can even show pictures of them online to potential buyers), real estate (pictures and descriptions of homes or property to a buyer anywhere in the world; can you imagine the time saved by doing preselecting online before your out-of-town client arrives?), recipes (low-fat, vegetarian, ethnic, grandma's Beehive cookies), costumes (period costume patterns e-mailed to interested buyers, Halloween costumes for non-sewing busy mothers), equipment, etc. There is a demand for hundreds of match up services.

Another good example is locating financing for new or expanding businesses. The most critical need for a new business is funding. Finding the financing for a business usually carries a good finder's fee (usually 1% - 10%). Databases of the groups that have money to invest (venture capitalists) have been put together. For a fee, you can feed the information about what a business needs into a database and be matched to venture capitalists who have expressed an interest in those types of businesses. Capital Source at **acgs@fsli.com** has a large database of venture capital sources. They will run a search for a modest fee. Think of the people you know who need money for the start-up or expansion of their businesses. There are many potential clients on the Internet who are looking for venture capital. Subscribe to business mailing lists (see Appendix 3). People who subscribe to these lists are interested in business topics. Some are actively searching for venture capital. You can do two things to develop your client base. You can e-mail directly to the person, tell him about your service and let him know how he can do business with you. Or you can post a well-worded ad which tells about your business and points clients to your WWW page or at least gives them an e-mail address where they can write for more information. Yes, this is advertising, but business listservs generally don't mind your posting this sort of information if you are a member of the list. It's best to check their policy before you post.

Here are a few ideas:

Auto Parts Database Catalog
Catalog Collections
Dating Match Service
Hobby Supplies
Period Costume Design
Seamstresses and Tailors
Real Estate Graphical Multiple Listing
Referral Services
Venture Capital Funding
Volunteer Projects

Chapter 30

 Service

Selling a service means you sell your time and/or expertise to do something for others that they either can't do or don't want to do for themselves. It makes more sense to pay someone else to do billing, track clients, or fix your refrigerator than to try to do it yourself. No, you don't need to be a highly trained technical professional. You only have to be able to provide something that others need and are willing to pay for. Recent statistics show that services now account for over half of the US economy. A much larger share of the consumer budget goes for services today than for consumable products. Tony Ferrullo in New Jersey, for example, runs a postcard mailing service for realtors, home improvement and swimming pool contractors. He uses software to generate a highly targeted mailing list. His clients are eager for his services because he can locate new customers for them while they are working with their present clients.

Another business opportunity might be available to you in the legal field. Many lawyers make their living in collections, but you can service collections without being a lawyer. With a good program, your computer can generate the letters required to push the collections all the way to court. If the collections do go to court, you need to have a good relationship with a collection's attorney. The two of you can make a good team. Join the local credit bureau and actually put credit notations on someone's credit report. (That is often more effective than going to court.) Some states require you to be licensed, but that normally isn't a very difficult or expensive process. Several packages exist that will give you samples of letters and paperwork in line with collection laws.

If collections don't sound interesting, have you ever written a business plan, resumé, employee manual, OSHA plan, safety plan, environmental impact statement or some other relatively complicated document? If you have, you have a skill that lots of little businesses and individuals will pay for. The computer makes changes in the basic documents easy. If you don't have experience, go to the business bulletin boards, look for categories such as Business Opportunities or subscribe to listservs. Both MIT and the University of Michigan maintain resource lists for small businesses. They can point you to programs to help budding entrepreneurs. There are companies who are looking for people who can draft documents for businesses. They may even tutor you until you learn, or at least they might give you sample documents and tell you how to learn more about them.

Someone with auditing skill could set up a business auditing utility bills (gas and electric) for people and companies. In a business, it is usual to find many errors in the billings made by the gas, electric and telephone companies. The savings recovered in the audits can be very substantial. You can charge to do the audit or take a piece of the savings as your pay. With a large company an auditor sometimes makes a full year's wage in several weeks. You do have to know the rates of the utility companies, and the process takes some time to learn, but the rewards can be big.

Use your fax/modem to go into business receiving and sending faxes like a local copy center. You could also equip your computer, or charge to equip other people's computers, to receive and send e-mail to and from others. You would be amazed at how many people are afraid of technology or think they are too old or too busy to learn. These people would rather pay for this service than make the Internet connections themselves. Many businesses and homes have a computer and printer, but no Internet connection. A computer and printer can be "turned into a Net connection" for a lot less than it costs to buy a fax machine. Here are a few other service ideas.

Amortization Schedules
Bockkeeping Service for Contractors, Professionals,

etc.

Budgeting Service
Billing Service for Contractors, Professionals, etc.
Collection Services
Company Newsletters
Custom Calendars, Pens, etc., for Businesses
Data Entry Service
Data Conversion Service
Delivery Service
Disk Advertising Service
Disk Copying and Formatting
Disk Based Information Service
Document Editing
Document Design
Elderly Alert Service
Electronic Clipping Service
Energy Consultant
Family Histories
Family Newsletters
Fax Services
Filing Service
Fulfillment House
Genealogy Compilation
Greeting Card Service
Hair Style Service
Job Location Services
Landscape Planning
Legal Filing
Legal Research
Mailing Label Addressing
Market Research
Medical Transcription

Meeting Scheduling
Menu Planning
Newsletters
Order Taking
Photographs Transferred to Computer
Postcard Mailing Service
Project Scheduling
Projecting
Record Keeping
Secretarial
Security Alert Service
Small Business Evaluation
Software Finder
Software Development
Sorting & Filing Service
Stock Market Analysis
Stock Market Investing
Survey Analysis Summary
Travel Guide
Vacation Site Information Guide
Valuing Collectibles
Video Text Screens
Word Processing

Chapter 31

Computer and Technical Services

A great business can be developed operating a computer or using some other technical skill. For instance, there are thousands of people who make a nice "extra" income performing desktop publishing. Many programs are readily available to set you up as a desktop publisher. Pick one and know it inside and out. See Appendix 7: Subject Related Internet Addresses. Competition is tough and making a full-time living at it is hard because competition can drive the price down, but it is always in demand.

Or you could use your knowledge of Internet marketing to help small businesses gain access to the power of the World Wide Web. You could start your own electronic mall and help clients develop home pages with hypertext links. Maintaining Web sites for other businesses, large and small, will be a profitable business. The time to get in on this one is NOW. The Internet is the marketing tool of the nineties, and more and more companies are discovering that they cannot afford to ignore it if they are going to compete. They will gladly pay you to take part in this market revolution.

A computer isn't enough to get you into the polling business. However, your computer coupled with a set of 900 telephone numbers can get you started. Use one 900 line for a positive vote and one line for a negative vote. The phone companies can get a 900 line set up for you, but it will be cheaper to go to a service bureau. For a couple hundred dollars you should be able to set up two 900 lines. Get a "partner" by going to local stores, radio stations, and newspapers; pick a controversial topic, and put your ad in the paper or on a radio station. You, of course, make money every time someone calls to register a vote. Share the money with your "partner." It's a great way to advertise if you do it right.

Before you or anyone buys a piece of real estate today, especially commercial real estate, the property should be scrutinized carefully. Several computer programs have been developed to accomplish the task. They take everything into account from the cost of the sewage service to the points you pay at the bank. If the analysis doesn't show the deal to be as good as the seller says it is, then you have concrete evidence to demand a lower price. If the analysis finds the deal is too good to pass up — buy. This analysis can be done for your own investments, or you can charge a price or "consulting fee" to brokers or other real estate investors. Your buyers can preselect interesting property by viewing pictures and descriptions over the

Internet. Busy clients will appreciate the service, and think of how much you will save by being able to narrow down the choices before you take your buyers on site. Travel and car expenses will go way down.

You could operate a scanning service. For this business, a scanner is required, along with the software which interfaces a computer with the scanner, but these are available for less than $1000. Businesses and individuals often have long documents that must be typed. If they are aware of your ability to scan (that is, to take type on a written page into a computer so that it can be edited and retyped), they will be happy to pay. Then you can transmit the information electronically. You should be able to scan their document faster and cheaper than they could pay someone to type the document. And remember, your clients can be anywhere in the world.

One rapidly growing company develops software for computer simulations of manufacturing and health care facilities. Imagine the money companies save if they simulate the new buildings, analyze traffic flow, and make design improvements before they do any actual building. Companies are looking for ways to be more cost-effective. If you can design and implement this kind of software, your service will always be in demand.

Here are a few more ideas to get you thinking about the kind of service your business could provide.

Computer Aided Design (CAD)
Computer Games
Computer Graphic Arts
Computer Portraits
Computer Repair
Computer Simulations
Computer Support Service
Computer Time Rental
Creating Home Pages for the Internet
Desk-top Publishing
Electronic Bulletin Board for Sales, Services or Marketing
Electronic Mail
Net Consultant
Personalized Books
Personalized Calendars
Personalized Cards
Personalized Letters
Polling
Real Estate Analysis
Scanning Services
Testing Software

Chapter 32

Keys for Success

We've given you a few of our ideas. You probably thought of many others as you've read through our suggestions. The keys to a successful business are:

- **Decide on a product or service that you really believe in.** One man developed a pamphlet on safety when he couldn't find a ready resource. He realized that others must need the same material, too. He direct mailed it to a list available in his field of work. Now he can advertise his pamphlet over the Internet to an international clientele.

- **Use what you already know**. The skills and talents that you presently have can be used to develop a business. A former buyer for a large department store decided to begin a home-based fashion consulting business so that she could stay at home near her two toddlers. She only needed a few samples to begin with, so her initial investment was minimal. She already knew her product. She loves providing a personal touch for her customers. Another advantage — she gets to buy all her own clothes at wholesale prices.

• **Consider the costs, risks, and potential return.** Do research on your product and its marketability. Run test ads on the Internet. It is very inexpensive. Run an ad on a commercial online service such as America Online, Prodigy or CompuServe. People who subscribe to an online service have already demonstrated that they are willing to spend money. Your potential return is limited only by the amount of time and energy you devote to your business.

• **Have pride in your work** and treat people with respect and dignity. Remember that you should choose your words carefully when you post on the bulletin boards or the Usenet newsgroups. Respond promptly to inquiries. Prepare carefully crafted answers. Work with clients to keep your product geared to their needs.

• **Be aware** that there is a small extremely vocal group on the Internet who are scratching and clawing to keep it a place accessible only to the academic community and computer geeks. They are known for their rudeness, their "flaming," their unwillingness to see what is happening to the Internet as a force for positive change in the world. It should be noted that they are sometimes willing to say and do things over the Internet that they would never do if they had to see their victims face-to-face. They hide behind the anonymity of their computer screens and express exaggerated rage and "unrighteous" indignation. What they seem to have conveniently forgotten is that First Amendment rights belong to all of us, and that they will benefit also from the changes taking place. The prices of goods and services will go down; quality will go up. Con artists will be exposed before they can do much damage. The education of the next generation will be better geared to individual needs. Services that all of us want to use will be more accessible. How do you deal with these vocal few? First, ignore them. Resist the temptation to respond in kind. "Flame wars" are childish and unproductive. Second, remember that the vast majority of Internet users are honest, hardworking people like you, and they aren't offended or even annoyed at advertisements whether they are in newspapers, magazines, flyers, or posted on the Internet.

• **Have a passion** for what you do. If you believe in your product and have a goal that you strongly desire to reach, you will be successful. Remember that these are not get-rich-quick schemes. Whatever effort and time you put into establishing your business will be worth it in terms of financial rewards. Moreover, if you enjoy what you are doing, your work will also be a source of tremendous personal satisfaction.

• **Have a vision** of the possibilities. This is a time for creative thinking. The Internet is being shaped and rewoven every day. You can have a hand in its development. The commercial implications of this new era are incalculable, and the time is ripe to become involved. It takes courage and vision to recognize what is happening and to be a part of it. Of course it may seem easier to maintain the status quo, but those, who wish to be at the forefront of these rapid changes, will courageously venture forth now. You can be a part of determining the way people do business in the coming years.

Conclusion

Realize that whether you choose to take action or not, the Information Superhighway is going to affect your life. It is the way of the future. Very soon you will find that the Internet, just like telephones and television, will be an indispensable part of civilized life. You will use it to talk to your friends, send letters, shop, get news, answer pressing questions, do research, consult experts, work with colleagues around the world, and solve problems. The Internet is here, and if you choose to become involved now, you can jump-start your future.

The Internet presents the greatest opportunity of our era. It represents a new and exciting world, and the commercial sector of this new world is ready to explode. Right now every business starting out on the Information Superhighway is starting from the same place. The playing field is level; size and reputations are unimportant. The Internet world is so new that there are no hard and fast rules, nor are experts able to predict the future. If you enter this world, you will be a pioneer. Pioneers enter new worlds, establish the conventions, set the standards, and make names for themselves as they explore and determine what will work. Pioneers courageously set the precedents.

To decide if you can successfully pioneer this world, consider the impact computers have already had on your life and on business. The commercial world is teaming with computer use. Computers are used in almost every aspect of the business world, because they make work easier, quicker, and more precise. Those who pioneered the computer world are truly the successful entrepreneurs of our era. The Internet holds similar promise for the business world. Now is the time to recognize the promise the Internet holds for the future and resolve to become a pioneer in this new world.

A pioneer needs to be familiar with the tools to use, and have the ability to creatively employ the tools in the new environment. The quickest way to learn how to use the Internet tools is to simply start playing with them. Take the plunge today. Jump in, and begin to experiment with the tools of the Internet. Use your creativity to think of ways to use these tools to leverage your time and talents. The Internet is constantly changing, and so are the most effective methods for doing business over the Internet. The best way to keep abreast of the rapid changes and utilize the incredible wealth and power of the Internet is to get on the Net and use it. Subscribe to the business lists in your areas of interest, observe what others are doing, and find your own way to do things better. Don't be afraid to examine new protocols and software and utilize all the available tools.

The opportunity to form an Internet business is knocking on your door. There are as many business opportunities as there are people and ideas. It doesn't matter what type of business you start, if you begin to explore this new market now, you will be one of the experts of the future. Perhaps the most important reason to use the Internet doesn't rest with speed, wealth, and opportunity, but with the intangible gift it

will give you to leverage your time, abilities and resources, freeing you to spend your time doing the things that will enrich your life — the things that you enjoy.

Now is the time to take advantage of the wealth of opportunities for doing business over the Internet. The costs of experimenting with an Internet business are minimal. This is an excellent way to begin testing your business ideas. It doesn't matter whether it is a new business or business that is changing directions. With work, imagination, and the courage to explore this new frontier, success can be yours.

Glossary

Access Provider - An organization that provides passage to the Internet.

Anonymous FTP - A procedure which permits the retrieval of files from a remote computer that the owner has made available for access without requiring an ID or a password.

BBS (Bulletin Board System) - An electronic posting system accessed by computer via a phone modem. Examples: large national systems such as America Online, Prodigy, CompuServe, and Delphi, as well as hundreds of smaller local systems. Such forums are operated under the same concept as a bulletin board in a local supermarket; messages are posted and can be read by interested parties.

Browser - A hypertext interface that enables movement between WWW documents. Examples include Mosaic and Netscape.

Client - Program that talks to the server.

Cyberspace - A term used to describe the network world of connected computers.

Dial-up - A type of Internet connection. A dial-up connection for access to the Internet through an Internet host by modem.

Discussion Groups - Organized groups that focus on discussing specific topics.

Domain - An administrative organizational category of the Internet.

Domain name - The name given to a specific area of the Internet for organizational purposes. The domain name is that part of an Internet address that falls after the @ symbol. If the Internet or e-mail address is ww@infodirect.com, the domain name is infodirect.

Download - The process of retrieving information and transferring it to specified computer files.

E-mail - Messages that are sent by computer to specific addresses. E-mail is short for "electronic mail."

E-mail address - A site which receives e-mail for a specific Internet user.

Electronic cash - Electronic currency available to move commerce over the Internet. It is a virtual currency having no guaranteed exchange rate.

Encryption - The process of coding information so that it can be kept confidential.

FAQs - Frequently Asked Questions. Lists of answers to frequently asked questions. FAQ collections help newcomers to familiarize themselves with the conventions of the Internet.

Flame - A mean or harsh Internet message, usually sent through e-mail or posted in a newsgroup.

Freeware - Free software available for distribution over the Internet. It can be downloaded and used without paying compensation.

FTP - (File Transfer Protocol) An Internet tool that allows users to retrieve a remote computer's files that the owner has made available.

Gopher - A menu-based Internet tool used for finding and retrieving files of all kinds.

GUI (Graphical User Interface) - A computer program that allows the user to interface with and move about on the World Wide Web in a point-and-click environment.

Home Page - An electronic storefront on the World Wide Web that is created using HyperText Markup Language.

Host - see Node.

Information Superhighway - A huge computer network connecting thousands of smaller networks worldwide.

Interface - Gateway or format which enables the user and the computer to communicate with one another.

Internet - A huge computer network connecting thousands of smaller networks worldwide.

InterNIC - The organization which has contracted to assign and keep track of all upper level domain names in the United States.

IP (Internet Protocol) - A set of technical rules and standards on the Internet for computer communication. Without protocols, computer networks could not exist, since the computers would not communicate with each other in an intelligible manner.

Listserv - A program that provides automatic processing of mailing lists.

Mailbots - A computer system or robot that responds automatically to certain incoming e-mail requests.

Mailing list - A moderated or automatic system for transmitting e-mail messages to a group of list subscribers.

Newsgroups - Groups which use the Internet to make their notices available on specific topics to interested readers who subscribe.

Newsreader - A client program which enables the user to read and manage messages posted on newsgroup bulletin boards.

Net -.A huge computer network connecting thousands of smaller networks worldwide. A shortened form of Internet.

Netiquette - Implied rules and customs for acceptable behavior on the Internet. Net + etiquette = netiquette.

Network - A group of computers that are connected in a way so that they can share information.

Node - A computer system that has a dedicated or full time connection to a network such as the Internet. It is sometimes called a host.

Path - The route that network traffic takes from its source to its destination. Sometimes called the route.

Posting - A single newsgroup message.

Protocol - A set of technical rules and standards for computer communication. Without protocols, computer networks could not exist, since the computers would not communicate with each other in an intelligible manner.

Server - A computer program that provides information on the Internet. Servers respond to queries from other computers.

Service provider - An organization that provides passage to the Internet.

Spamming - The act of sending or posting the same message to as many newsgroups as possible without regard to topic of discussion.

Telnet - A system that allows a computer to control at least a portion of a remote computer. It is commonly used to provide off-site access to such services as automated library catalogs or BBSs around the world.

URL (Uniform Resource Locator) - An addressing system for Internet documents, including World Wide Web home pages. A URL contains the type of server, where the server is located and where on that server a specific document is found.

UNIX - A computer operating system with powerful networking features. Much of the Internet has been built on a foundation of UNIX technology.

Usenet - The Usenet is an informal system that uses the Internet to exchange "news" for newsgroups.

Veronica - A tool for searching out Gopher-accessible information. An acronym for "Very Easy Rodent-Oriented Net-wide Index to Computerized Archives."

WAIS - A system for searching through the contents of indexed documents on the Internet.

World Wide Web (WWW) - The World Wide Web is a system of interconnected computer sites that are primarily linked through hypertext. Web sites can include multimedia forms, such as graphics, input fields, audio, and video.

Appendices

Appendix 1: Demographics and Statistics

CERN
http://info.cern.ch/

GVU Center at Georgia Tech
Majordomo@cc.gatech.EDU

Internet Domain Survey
http://www.nw.com/zone/WWW/top.html

Internet Society
ftp://ftp.isoc.org/

John Quarterman
gopher://gopher.tic.com/00/matrix/news/v4/
faq.406

Merits NIC Stats and Plots
http://www.cc.gatech.edu/gvu/stats/NSF/
merit.html

Michigan Business School
http://www.umich.edu@sgupta/hermes.htm

Appendix 2: Places to Advertise on the Internet

Apollo Advertising
   http://apollo.co.uk/home.html
   free online advertisements

Branch Information Services
   http://branch.com

Electronic Mall on the Internet
   http://www.imall.com/ads/ads.html

Entrepreneur Net
   http://cyberzine.org/html/Entrepreneur/
   enetpage.html

Epages
   http://ep.com

The Exchange
   http://www.iea.com/~adlinkex
   gopher.iea.com
   ftp.iea.com

First Virtual
   http://www.fv.com

The Global On-line Directory

http://cityscape.co.uk/gold/

ICNet
http://www.ic.net

InfoPost
http://www.infopost.com

Internet Business Pages
info@msen.com

Internet Marketing, Inc
http://cybersight.com/cgi-bin/imi/s?main.gmml

Internet Plaza
http://storefron.xor.com/

Internet Shopkeeper
http://www.ip.net/shops/

MagNet
e-mail to support@omega.intercalm.com
1-800-303-9211

Netcenter
http://netcenter.com

Netsurfer Marketplace
http://www.netsurf.com

Network Wizards
  http://www.catalog.com/catalog/top.html

Openmarket
  http://www.openmarket.com

SuperNet Interactive Services
  http://www.success.net

The Tarheel Mall
  e-mail to Netmar@netcom.com

Virtual Advertising (Adfx Mall)
  http://www.shore.net/~adfx/top.html

VirtualNet Consulting
  e-mail to: services@virtual.net

Appendix 3: Business and Business Related Listservs

The List of Marketing Lists
nsns.com/MouseTracks/tloml.html

Directmar
bfb@world.std.com.
Send e-mail to majordomo@world.std.com

Free-Market
Send e-mail to listserv@ar.com

Globmkt
Send e-mail to listserv@ukcc.uky.edu

Inet-Marketing
Send e-mail to listproc@einet.net

Newprod
Send e-mail to majordomo@world.std.com

Market-L
Send e-mail to majordomo@mailer.fsu.edu

Ritim-L
Send e-mail to listserv@uriacc.uri.edu

Business-related Electronic Newsletters:

Digital Future
> e-mail to fyi@marketplace.com
> gopher marketplace.com

Ideas DIGest ONLINE
> http://www.wimsey.com/~idig/

Internet Advertising Review
> e-mail to mstrange@fonorola.net   Subject:
> Review2

New on the Net
> http://directory.net/netinfo

Ways Biz Magazine
> http://www.cyberplex.com/CyberPlex/
> WaysMag.html

Appendix 4: FTP Sites

rtfm.mit.edu

archive.umich.edu

sumex-aim.stanford.edu

oak.oakland.edu

ftp.sura.net

quartz.rutgers.edu

wuarchive.wustl.edu

Appendix 5: Bulletin Board Systems that Allow Advertising

G.L.O.B.I.E. (telnet net1.intsev.com)

G.O.D. (telnet acadh2.isisnet.com)

Magnus Online (telnet online.magnus.com)

Odyssey (telnet odyssey.ody.com)

Online Computer Distribution (telnet main.oncomdis.on.ca)

Pacifier Online Data Service (telnet pods.pacifier.com)

Appendix 6: Sites Related to Tax Issues

Frank McNeil's Income Tax Information
     ftp://ftp.netcom.com/pub/ft/ftmexpat/
     taxsites.htm

     ftp ftp.netcom.com/pub/html2text/taxsites.txt

Home page of the IRS
     http://www.ustreas.gov/treasury/bureaus/irs/
     irs.html

mailing list:
     send e-mail to *lasser@acc.fau.edu* and
     subscribe to ATTAX-L mailing list

Misc. Taxes. FAQ
     gopher gopher.metronet.com

Newsgroup
     misc.taxes

Network Wizards
     http://www.nw.com

Appendix 7: Subject Related Internet Addresses

General:

Internet Lists:

Currency Exchanges
> http://www.ora.com/cgibin/ora/currency

Internet Services List
> newsgroup alt.bbs.internet Article: 5879
> e-mail to yanoff@alpha2csd.uwm.edu
> This list is a must.

Yahoo
> http://akebono/stanford.edu/yahoo

Business:

Business Resource Center
> http://www.kcilink.com/sbhc/

Business Resources
> gopher gopher.nijenrode.nl

Commercial Sites Index
> http://www.directory.net

Cyberpreneurs Guide to the Internet
http://asa.ugl.lib.umich.edu/chdocs/
cyberpren%3aschwilk.html

gopher://una.hh.lib.umich.edu/00/inetdirsstacks/
cyberpren%3aschwilk

Economic BBS
telnet ebb.stat-usa.gov
gopher una.hh.lib.umich.edu

Entrepreneurs on the Web
http://sashimi.wwa.com/~notime/eotw/
EOTW.html

IndustryNet
http://www.industry.net/guide.html

Internet Business Center
http://www.tig.com/IBC/

Small Business Administration
gopher://www.sbaonline.gov:70/00/

Trafford, Ltd.
http://cityscape.co.uk/cgi-bin/
dat2html?file=2609

Wimsey Corporation
http://www.wimsey.com

Newsgroups
alt.business
alt.business.import-export
alt.business.internal.audit
alt.business.misc
alt.business.multi-level
biz.general
biz.jobs.offered
biz.marketplace.noncomputer
biz.misc
biz.next.newprod.
misc.business.facilitators
misc.entrepreneurs
misc.entrepreneurs.moderated
misc.forsale
misc.wanted
misc.invest

Desktop Publishing:
Internet Desktop Publishing Jumplist
> http://www.cs.purdue.edu/homes/gwp/dtp/
> dtp.html

> ftp.dopig.uab.edu   /info/pagemakr/faq
> ftp wuarchive.wustl.edu /doc/misc/pagemakr

The Scanning FAQ
http://www.dopig.uab.edu/dopigpages/FAQ/
The-Scan-FAQ.html

Newsgroups:
alt.aldous.freehand
alt.aldous.pagemaker

Diet and Nutrition:
Fatfree Recipe Archive
ftp ftp.geod.emr.ca/pub/Vegetarian/Recipes/
FatFree
FDA
gopher zeus.esusda.gov 70

Arizona Health Science Library
http://amber.medlib.arizona.edu/nutrition.html

Ohio State University Medical Center
gopher gizmo.freenet.columbus.oh.us 70

World Guide to Vegetarianism
http://catless.ncl.ac.uk/vegetarian

ftp rtfm/mit.edu/pub/usenet/news.answers/
vegetarian/guide

Genealogy:
CLIO—National Archives Gopher/WWW
http://www.nara.gov

Genealogy Home Page
http://www.ftp.cac.psu.edu/~saw/
genealogy.html

Internet Roots Surname list
http:/genealogy.emcee.com/

National Genealogical Society BBS
modem call to 703-528-2612

Roots-L mailing list

University of Toledo Gopher
gopher alpha.cc.utoledo.edu

Newsgroup:
alt.genealogy

Legal Issues:
Asset Protection and License Preparation System
http://www.legalees.com/legalees.html

Copyright information
gopher marvel.loc.gov

Copyright laws and FAQs
> ftp rtfm.mit.edu/pub/usenet/news.answers/law/
> Copyright-FAQ

Cornell University Law School
> http://www.law.cornell.edu//usc17/
> overview.html

Real Estate:

CORA& Sime Home Page
> http://www.bendnet.com/cosime.html

Four Circles Realty
> http://www.internet-is.com/re/

HomeBuyer's Fair Welcome
> http://www.homefair.com/

Homes and Land Welcome Page
> http://www.homes.com/Welcome.html

Global Electronic Marketing Service
> http://www.gems.com/realestate/index.html

Real Estate Showcase
> http://www.xmission.com/~mg/realty.html

Virtual HomeFront
> http://www.PrimeNet.Com:80/homes/

Newsgroup:

misc.invest.real-estate

Mailing Lists

Email: listserve@property.com

Commercial real estate: include
"subscribe commercial realestate <your
email address>"

Residential real estate: include
"subscribe residential realestate <your
email address>"

Index

Index

A

Access providers 47, 48, 49
Advertising 40, 45, 56, 89, 140, 163
Advertising 27, 45, 46, 52, 73, 84, 103, 123, 124, 151, 156
Archive 108
Audio conferencing 58

B

BBS 130
Browser 85, 92, 118
Bulletin Board System 34, 100
Business Ideas 133, 176

C

Chat 49, 58, 129, 143
Commercial online service 49, 170
Commercial sites 95
Company Image 31
Cost Savings 43
Customer support 75, 116, 124
CyberCash 77
Cyberspace 25, 45, 70, 90, 91, 93, 97, 107, 124, 128

D

Demographic 17, 23
DigiCash 77
Domain name 25, 26, 27, 28, 100
Download 44, 60, 67, 79, 85, 92, 103, 116, 118, 138

E

E-mail 57, 71, 99, 100
E-mail address 104
Education 56, 60, 130, 138, 143, 144, 145, 146, 171

Electronic brochures 40, 76
Electronic Cash 77, 85, 86
Electronic Mail 75, 76, 168
Electronic newsletter 115
Encryption 82, 86
Entrepreneur 100

F

File Transfer Protocol 49, 113
Flame 171
Freeware 111
Frequently Asked Questions 104, 116, 143
FTP 49, 63, 72, 92, 93, 111, 113, 114, 115, 116, 117, 118, 131
Future 18, 19, 27, 33, 48, 55, 58, 75, 128, 173, 174, 175

G

Games 122, 129, 130, 151, 168
Genealogy 138, 139, 141, 162
Globalization 37
Gopher
    49, 72, 92, 93, 103, 107, 108, 109, 110, 111, 115, 117, 131

H

History 7, 15, 37, 122, 145
Home page 40, 45, 46, 77, 78, 79, 93, 94, 95, 97, 109, 138
HTML 51, 94, 95
HyperText Markup Language 51, 94, 95

I

Information Superhighway 7, 8, 21, 48, 60, 70, 78, 151, 173
Interface 51, 92, 121
Internet Relay Chat 58, 143
Internet Tools 43, 45, 63, 90, 174
InterNIC 25
IRC 57, 58, 129, 143

L

Listserv 100, 102, 103, 104, 105
Low Overhead 47

M

Mail Lists 100
Mailbots 101
Management 147, 148, 149, 154
Market Research 44, 162
Marketing 69, 81, 151, 153, 168
Merchant Accounts 82, 84
Mosaic 21, 51, 52, 85, 89, 92, 113

N

Netiquette 70
Netscape 51, 52, 85, 89, 92, 113, 118, 119
Network 7, 26, 86
Newsgroups
    40, 69, 72, 104, 121, 122, 123, 124, 125, 139, 151, 170
Newsreader 121, 123

O

Online Access 48
Online Business 55
Online Providers 72

P

Protocol 49, 70, 92, 111, 113

R

Research 65, 146, 162

S

Savings 32, 43, 56, 57, 161
Server 48, 94, 111, 118, 121
Service 146, 149, 153, 157, 159, 161, 162, 163, 168
Shareware 116, 129, 139
Size and Growth 21
Small Business 100, 149, 163
Spamming 123, 124
Storefront 51, 90
Survey 163

T

Telecommuting 63
Telnet 49, 72, 92, 128
Tools 38, 43, 45, 47, 49, 63, 71, 72, 77, 85, 87,
    89, 90, 92, 174, 175
Top-level Domain 26

U

UNIX 51, 86
Usenet 121, 123, 170

V

Venture Capital 156, 157
Video Conferencing 43, 58, 63, 64

W

World Wide Web
    21, 40, 45, 49, 72, 78, 91, 92, 93, 97, 102, 103, 109, 138, 165
WWW 45, 78, 91, 92, 95, 125, 131, 156